Praise for *Block Breaker*

"In *Block Breaker*, Brian challenges the assumption that *Minecraft* is simply a game. Readers are asked to consider thinking beyond pedagogical tradition and convention. Brian makes a strong case for moving beyond compliance to tap into students' potential with authentic, student-driven activities and approaches to learning."

—David Carruthers,
educator, learning coordinator, blogger, edtech enthusiast

"You don't have to know coding or *Minecraft* to read this book. It's more about good twenty-first-century approaches to teaching: giving up the idea of teacher as holder and imparter of knowledge, moving to 'knowing the curriculum and recognizing teachable moments,' and being vulnerable enough to learn with your students while ensuring they are fulfilling curriculum expectations. Brian offers a good launching point for teachers looking to change their approach to meeting student needs. He reminds us we need to challenge the way things have always been done."

—Lori DiMarco,
superintendent, curriculum leadership and innovation;
and academic ICT, Toronto Catholic District School Board

"Brian's passion for authentic learning experiences that will build lifelong success for our next generation is evident throughout *Block Breaker.* With clear classroom examples to implement immediately and encouragement to break from traditional teaching models, this book is sure to be a useful resource for many educators."

—Becky Keene,
director, insight2execution

"Brian's new book *Block Breaker* takes an exceptionally astute second look at the pedagogical structures and the mindsets adopted by successful learners and educators when infusing coding in authentic and engaging cross-curricular computational thinking inquiries. This and his first book *Code Breaker* are must-reads for educators venturing into computational thinking and coding at any level."

—Keith Strachan,
learning technology support, Winnipeg School Division

"With *Block Breaker,* Brian continues to challenge us to explore beyond the one-size-fits-all method of education in preparing our students for real-world experiences. Brian shares his passion to expand our educational mindset, increase opportunity for our students in inquiry-based projects, and look beyond the confines of traditional practices. If you are seeking to be creative and innovative in your teaching, then this is the book for you!"

—Joshua Stamper,
administrator, blogger,
and host of *Aspire: The Leadership Development Podcast*

"*Block Breaker* will wind you through a path that explores mathematical viewpoints, teaching strategies, student engagement, and the deep purpose for why we teach. And for anyone who has said that *Minecraft* is a waste of time (I know I once did), *Block Breaker* can help you view new tools of engagement, like *Minecraft*, as time well spent. Give this book a chance and give your teaching practices a good, long look. In mathematics and beyond, we can all become Block Breakers."

—Denis Sheeran,
author, speaker, math educator

"Where *Code Breaker* started us on a journey into coding and computational thinking, *Block Breaker* plunges you into an adventure of teaching practices, philosophies, and how today's learners see the world. With Brian's combination of resources, models, and insights, we can only hope that the *Breaker* series enters the world of epic trilogies!"

—Kyle Kitchen,
educator, creator of Kinders Who Code

"*Block Breaker* provides amazing resources for any educator to implement fun and engaging STEM ideas through *Minecraft*. It also continues to challenge teachers' standard lesson designs and pedagogy. The more you read the more you are amazed at the possibilities for our students and how bright our future will look!"

—Jonathan So,
TEDx speaker, educator, and lover of bow ties

"Brian Aspinall continues to inspire by encouraging us to think beyond traditional teaching and assessment methods. While *Code Breaker* emphasized the importance of computational thinking, *Block Breaker* pushes us further by taking a closer look at best practices, including tried and true examples, to unleash student potential."

—Annick Rauch,
French immersion educator, learner, mom

"This is not just a book on how to make your classroom *Minecraft*astic. Yes, Brian has a treasure chest full of *Minecraft* ideas. But he also digs into the role that playing, grades, devices, listening, empowerment, rules, and creativity should have in our classrooms today. And that's kid-tastic!"

—Chris Woods,
teacher, tinkerer, and host of the *STEM Everyday* podcast

"Brian keeps effective pedagogy and practice at the forefront of *Block Breaker*. His storytelling offers authentic tasks and tools for differentiated learning that will push today's educator to challenge the status quo by offering solutions in how to break traditional educational mindsets. A great read for any educator who wants to do what is best for kids."

—Joanne Borges,
lead learner and school administrator

"In *Block Breaker*, Brian pushes our thinking about traditional, often ineffective models used in schools and offers innovative approaches and beyond, that support both student engagement and empowerment. Brian also inspires educators to explore and be curious as learners themselves!"

—Shauna Cornwell,
enrichment and innovation consultant, Winnipeg

"*Block Breaker* does more than just talk about *Minecraft* in the math class; it gets to the root of the technology debate, addressing the significance of giving students authentic tasks, advocating for collaboration, and stressing the importance of continuous feedback for growth. His words are an important reminder that we do not cover curriculum as educators; we empower learners to uncover it."

—Jen Giffen (@VirtualGiff),
educator, podcaster, edtech enthusiast

"*Block Breaker* flips the way you think about how gaming can be used within the classroom and its positive impact on student learning. This book is an absolute way to encourage educators to reflect on their own practices when it comes to incorporating engaging ways to teach math."

—Elaine Higa,
East Hawaii early literacy resource teacher

"In his new book *Block Breaker*, Brian openly and creatively explores the notion of breaking away from traditional teaching, moving toward building a foundation for modern learning and pedagogy in the age of digital technologies. Brian again inspires his readers to play hard in 'hard play' and explore technology as a way to rediscover learning in the modern world."

—Leigh Cassell,
education and innovation consultant, founder and president, Digital Human Library, founder, Live Learning Canada

"Once again, Brian has turned his passion for coding in education into an easy-to-follow guide for all teachers. *Block Breaker* provides specific lesson plans for teachers to implement in their classrooms now to get their students coding and challenge their thinking. Brian's ability to incorporate math concepts into coding continues to impress me. Every teacher needs to add this book to their educational library."

—Alice Aspinall,
mathematics teacher, author of *Everyone Can Learn Math*

"This book is not about *Minecraft*; it's not about the tool. It's about the pedagogy and a shift in how we think about education. *Block Breaker* is a must-read, and when paired with *Code Breaker*, you should prepare to have your educational world... well, broken... in the best way possible!"

—Alicia Ray (@iluveducating),
lead digital learning and media innovation facilitator, creator of #DBC50Summer and #DBCBookBlogs, lifelong lover of learning, mom

"Focusing on teaching practices, pedagogy, and thought leadership, Brian has constructed a book that helps raise the bar and close the gap in achievement for all students. Reach every student and let Brian show you the way...we dare ya!"

—Lee Martin,
daredevil educator, speaker, founder, risk-taker

"In *Block Breaker,* Brian gives an impassioned message for educators. It is not about the newest tech or app. But rather it is how you approach working with students. By inspiring and empowering students through choice and creativity, you will open up doors of learning with them in ways that you never thought possible."

—Richard Roberts,
learning technologies consultant, Winnipeg

"Mr. Aspinall has created a snapshot of a positive, progressive, ever-changing classroom, where all are engaged, and where all have something to teach and learn. The personal interviews, classroom experiences, and easy-to-use lesson plans challenge those who haven't yet tried coding to step up and give it a try. I am thankful to have Mr. Aspinall as a mentor to my own classroom coding adventure and feel my students have definitely benefited from the skill development."

—Laura Deeves (@LauraDeeves),
teacher with CDSBEO and Microsoft innovative expert educator

"My teacher life drastically changed when I met Brian a few years ago. I had never worked with coding or *Minecraft* before but started using both immediately after we met. *Block Breaker* is special to me because it's that first inspirational meet in a book! I hope it inspires and encourages educators everywhere to do more—for themselves and their students."

—Katja Borregaard,
lifelong learner, educator, and *Minecraft* mentor

"Initially, with *Code Breaker,* and now with his second book *Block Breaker,* Brian Aspinall has taken the criteria for the twenty-first-century student and made them accessible to all in a fun and engaging way! Brian's books are not only insightful and user-friendly, but they make technology no longer seem frightening but a classroom tool that is exciting and possible for educators and students alike. The expertise he passes on to his readers is the perfect building block for discovery education, where educators and students are learning together, and that is a beautiful thing!"

—Kim Gray,
mathematics educator, newbie coder (thanks to Brian)

"This book inspires us to see that all spaces are learning spaces—learning doesn't begin when students walk into the classroom and end when they leave. It reminds us, as educators, to know our curriculum first. Then we are equipped to trust our students to demonstrate their understanding of the curriculum in ways that are meaningful to them."

—Mistene S. Clapp,
innovation and technology support for learning teacher

"As an educator who has used *Minecraft* in the classroom, I can relate firsthand the power of *Minecraft* as a collaborative, creative, and transformational tool. Aspinall's new book is so much more than a book about *Minecraft;* it explores concepts like spiraling, gradeless classrooms, STEAM, design thinking, and coding. Aspinall's book is a powerful read for all teachers interested in modern pedagogy and amplifying student voices."

—Vickie Morgado, MEd,
teacherpreneur, blogger, presenter, change agent

"Brian's unparalleled passion for making a movement to provide students of all ages and abilities opportunities to use computational thinking to enhance learning is evident and inspiring in *Block Breaker.*"

—Nycol Didcote,
elementary French immersion teacher,
MEd inclusive education student

"Math education has not only seen its day, but at this point, has *well* lived past it. I'm glad to see I'm not the only one who thinks that disruptive education is not only a way, but *the* way to finally give math ed the makeover it so desperately needs. *Block Breaker* is kind of like one of those riveting home reno shows—but for coding! And *everyone* loves a good home reno show, am I right?!"

—Vanessa Vakharia,
founder of The Math Guru, author of *Math Hacks*,
and rockstar ("Goodnight, Sunrise")

"Brian challenges the comfort zone in teaching what we are familiar with to supporting students with the skills and supports they need to strive toward their goals. It's time to rethink how learning experiences are created for all learners. *Block Breaker* dives into the world of *Minecraft* to create, be curious, and build, reminding us that inspiration can be found anywhere."

—Zélia Capitão-Tavares,
Toronto District School Board hybrid teacher, digital lead learner

BLOCK BREAKER

Building Knowledge and Amplifying Student Voice One Block at a Time!

BRIAN ASPINALL

Block Breaker

Published by Dave Burgess Consulting, Inc.
San Diego, CA
http://daveburgessconsulting.com

Cover Design by Genesis Kohler
Editing and Interior Design by My Writers' Connection

Library of Congress Control Number: 2019931726
Paperback ISBN: 978-1-949595-24-6
Ebook ISBN: 978-1-949595-25-3

First Printing: March 2019

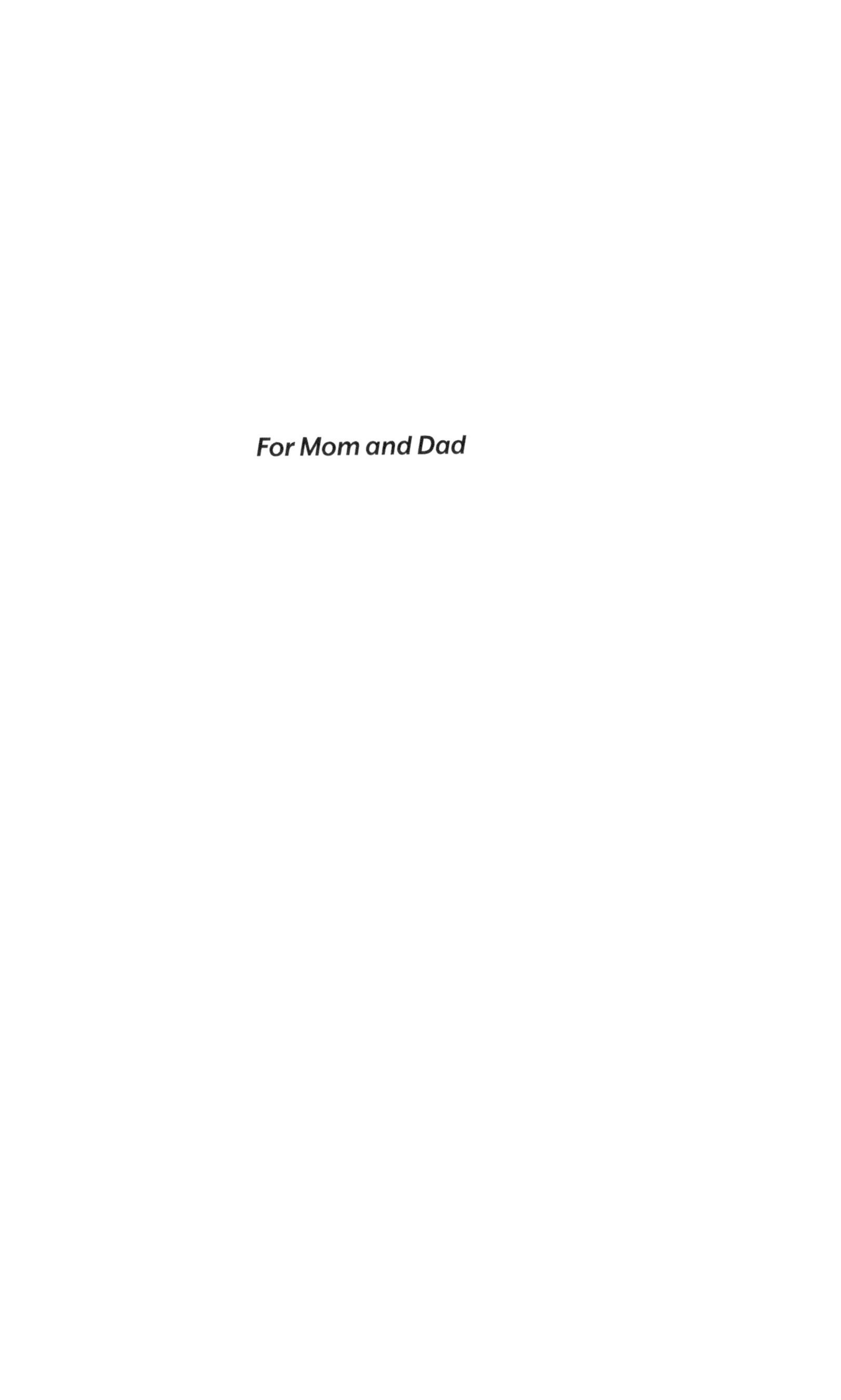

For Mom and Dad

Contents

Foreword

0 0 0 0 0 0 0 0

In 2013 I crossed off one of my bucket list items when I attended the SXSW Music Festival in Austin, Texas. Since then I have been back to Austin two more times. Austin is easily my favorite city in North America. The frequency that people are dialed into is off the normal bandwidth that the rest of society operates in. Sure, Austin is about music. But it is more than that. There is a sense of purpose toward the arts. Creativity is treasured. The more originality and imagination are pushed, the higher the currency of those efforts. There really is no edge. There are no boundaries of exploration in music, food, and general lifestyle philosophies. The motto "Keep Austin Weird" is a testament to how Austinites live and play. Weird? Weird is good.

You know what else is amazingly weird?

Mathematics.

> ***There is nothing as dreamy and poetic,***
> ***nothing as radical, subversive,***
> ***and psychedelic as mathematics.***
> *—Paul Lockhart*

Every descriptive word in that quote (which many math educators have figuratively tattooed to themselves) is the mathematical experience that awaits everyone. And while mathematics patiently waits to be courted—to be wooed by the most romantic ideas of numbers and patterning—very few come knocking on the door.

That's because that door does not exist inside of education. The mathematical door that is inside most K–12 schools leads to a wobbly onramp, filled with potholes, leading to a mathematical trespass that is narrow, uninviting, and deathly boring. An anxious journey is usually all that awaits.

So where is this magical and mysterious door? Where does one find the land of mathematical milk and honey? Although there is no prescribed route to find this oasis, there is one thing I am certain of: it will never be found in the emotionally parched conditions of classrooms that view math in arid, practical benchmarks of "student success," all the while quizzing and testing kids into that state of math anxiety that schools themselves create and then offer snake oil treatments. Sorry, but we are not running a pink elephant petting zoo here.

Things need to be said. Comfort zones destabilized. Disruptive ideas fertilized.

Going with the flow of this book, it is high time to break things—especially if they are broken.

I met Brian Aspinall back in September 2017 at The Fields Institute at The University of Toronto. We both spoke on the topic of Artificial Intelligence in Math Education and participated in a panel discussion. We listened attentively to each other that day. We, strangely, continued listening to each other on Twitter. I say "strangely" because our direct communication remained somewhat dormant—mostly because of being very busy with so many projects. We became friends on Facebook to strengthen the social media bond, but still, we were at the mercy of time to go beyond the cyber connections built on our Fall meeting of 2017.

Although there was no communication beyond some supportive words/likes of tweets, one thing was pretty clear: we were kindred spirits in trying to break a system that was never built for creativity, freedom, and empathy. Eventually the planets lined up, and we made time to talk. The topic was the obvious need we see for all of us as educators to intertwine our energies and visions and dismantle a system of learning that is failing. It may not be failing the adults that want control and authority over students, but it sure as hell is failing students, who see the learning as a long joyless trek of impersonal and meaningless busy work—thoroughly devoid of any personal inflections from them and their teachers.

Inert knowledge is not only useful; it is dangerous.
—Alfred North Whitehead, Aims of Education, 1929

Brian and I care about deep, human connections that honour the bluntest of truths. If going "rogue" means caring about the social, emotional, and intellectual well-being of students, then colour us with the brightest red crayon you can find. This is how peppered our first, real conversation was. And very quickly, Brian and I agreed that talking about learning mathematics in the freest and most disruptive ways would have to be the path—of no turning back—that had to be reached.

From a certain point onward, there is no turning back. That point must be reached.
—Franz Kafka

Brian and I are not turning back. We are like happy kids, skipping almost, meeting our kindred spirits that have become our tribe. We are also intensely serious about installing mathematical play that is robust and rich. That, specifically, is what we are not going to turn back from.

The "Rabbit Hole" will be a chapter in my upcoming book, *Math Recess,* to be co-authored with Dr. Chris Brownell, from Fresno,

California (another happy disruptor). In it, I take a deep journey into why this magical entrance to mathematics will aid in the overdue reconstruction and rehumanization of learning mathematics. And yes, we must first break the old, but disruptive vision also requires following the wisdom imparted by the twentieth-century architect, designer, author, and futurist, Buckminster Fuller:

> ***You never change things by fighting the existing reality. To change something, build a new model that makes the old model obsolete.***

Demanding a new model of math education does not mean we must sacrifice rigor. On the contrary, the vision Brian and I share wildly colours math education—outside the lines even—with creativity, curiosity, and courage. Current math education is deathly boring and disconnected. And then, to heap non-stop testing on top of this mess? No one should be surprised that students are checking out earlier and earlier when it comes to being interested in mathematics. Badges of anxiety and low self-esteem are the souvenirs that many depart with.

The only way to save math education from itself is to let it implode—after a more vibrant and colourful illumination of mathematical exploration is created. And it starts where mathematics started—with numbers. Not just counting and mathematical operations. These are key foundational pieces that will stay intact. It goes further, following the historical narrative of deep and wondrous exploration into the patterns and mysteries of numbers. We are talking about number theory.

While the word "theory" might seem off-putting and perhaps dry, nothing could be further from the truth—in spite of many university courses centred around this branch of mathematics. You see, the portal for entering the weird and wacky world of mathematics is the magic of numbers. Weird? Wacky? Magic? Are these words ever associated with mathematics in schools? Rarely. Yet these words are exactly the ones that will chaperone the curious traveler through the timeless enchantment with numbers—the rabbit hole of mathematics. And the journey can begin—should begin—in elementary school. To be more specific, prime numbers.

Just like kids learn their alphabet, primary school children should learn about prime numbers. But not in the passive way of learning about them, like they do most of mathematics. Kids should explore the sandbox of numbers—and find them on their own! There is no better way to develop factual fluency in mathematics than by finding the primes.

Playing with prime numbers is akin to the timeless image of Alice kneeling down on the ground and peeking into the rabbit hole. There was no stopping Alice, and there will be no stopping kids who start to play with primes. They are ready to experience the wonderland of numbers—number theory! It's time to let our kids get weird—The "Austin" of mathematics awaits.

Sunil Singh, @Mathgarden
mathematical jester and author
Pi of Life: The Hidden Happiness of Mathematics
Math Recess: Playful Learning for The Age of Disruption

Hello, World!

0 0 0 0 0 0 0 0

"NEXT TIME YOU ARE AFRAID TO SHARE IDEAS, REMEMBER SOMEONE ONCE SAID IN A MEETING 'LET'S MAKE A FILM WITH A TORNADO FULL OF SHARKS!'"

I first saw this comment in a tweet from Jon Acuff (@JonAcuff) in 2015 when *Sharknado 3* was on the horizon. It has resurfaced again on social media since *The Last Sharknado* was released in summer 2018. If you're counting, that makes six *Sharknado* movies. Six.

What Acuff's simple, yet profound, comment suggests to me is that any idea has potential for success when it's supported by good marketing, millennial engagement, and some social media know-how. If that's true, the questions I want to explore are how can we, as educators, tap into these elements of marketing, engagement, and social media? How well do we know our students? What do we know about the social spaces in which they live? And perhaps most importantly, if all spaces are learning spaces, how can we use different types of spaces to create engaging, interactive, and relevant learning opportunities?

Let me give you an example: countless young people are spending hours creating and consuming content on YouTube. As of 2014, YouTube had over 48 billion views on homemade *Minecraft* content. Typically, this content is created by kids without adults asking them to do so, and clearly, kids want to watch this content.

If you aren't into *Minecraft* or YouTube, you might be thinking, what a waste of time! But because you're reading this book, my guess is that you already have an inkling of how powerful learning can be when we combine our lessons with our students' passions. Imagine, for example, how engagement might increase if you used a video made by students (on their own time) to teach math concepts about proportional reasoning in *Minecraft*. Imagine teaching geography by tracking statistics about visitors to their videos, using YouTube analytics. Imagine having students make predictions about bias and learn financial literacy by monetizing on YouTube! We are literally only scratching the surface with potential possibilities. But before we get too far ahead, let's take a walk down memory lane.

In a world that changes overnight, we must teach students the only strategy guaranteed to fail is not trying something new.

#BlockBreaker

This story begins with my first teaching assignment in an intermediate school (you might call it middle school). Right from the beginning, a veteran colleague warned me that "grade eight teachers run a tight ship." To this day, I'm not clear what that means, but I interpreted the comment based on my own experience in grade eight: We sat in quiet rows. For the first time in my education, the teacher was a man. He wore a tie, and I was afraid to make eye contact with him. Intimidated or not, I thoroughly enjoyed my grade eight year. While setting up my first classroom, I was determined to mimic his.

Like his, my first was a classroom built on control and compliance. I made the seating plan based on nothing but students' names. I posted a list of classroom rules written in a "thou shalt not" manner:

- No chewing gum.
- Put your hand up to speak.
- Do not talk over others.
- Don't do this.
- Don't do that.
- I am in charge.

I have changed a lot since that first year. I still use the word *compliance*, but it holds a different meaning for me these days. To me compliant students are engaged and invested in their learning. Compliant students follow the culture and norms of a school while engaging in rich tasks that help better the community. Compliant students use the washroom when they need to and typically rush back to class for FOMO (fear of missing out).

Compliant students are curious problem solvers with ideas and thoughts they wish to explore authentically.

And quite often, this kind of learning and exploration involves making noise. The more I change my definition of compliance, the less talking I do in class. Long gone are the days when I would stand and deliver curriculum, like a UPS driver rushing from activity to activity to make sure I had covered the curriculum. In those days, my preconceived need for marks (grades) drove my instruction. Which meant I handed out and graded a lot of worksheets. Why was I so concerned with filling a markbook? I thought it made me a good teacher. What did that prove and who did I even show it to? Nothing and no one.

Teaching grade eight that year, I felt the pressure of preparing my students for high school. I expected them to take copious notes, excel at tests, and do hours of homework. In my classroom (both as a student and as a first-year teacher), good students were defined by spouting answers quickly and accurately, particularly in math. Students who did not complete homework earned detention. Period. It didn't matter why the homework wasn't finished. Today I understand the equity concerns with regards to homework. Perhaps those students who never finished didn't do so because they did not know how and had nowhere to turn for help. Perhaps those students were babysitting siblings all night or participating in school clubs or events. But back then, regardless of the reason, my immediate response was, "No recess for you!" (Imagine taking away a much needed break—for us both—and the damage I caused to my relationship with those students!)

It is okay to be where you are.

It is not okay to stay there.

Long gone are the days when assigning piles of homework made me a good teacher. Yes, I believed that once. (If you or your administrators still think homework equates to good teaching, read *Ditch That Homework* by Matt Miller and Alice Keeler. You'll be enlightened!)

Long gone are the days in which note-taking was the *most important skill*—as if copying words from the board meant students actually understood the material. Sure, taking notes is important, but teaching kids to summarize information significantly outweighs the effectiveness of copying notes from the board word for word. Sketchnoting—which uses limited words—can be an exceptionally helpful way to organize thoughts and ideas.

Long gone are the quiet rows of desks, and I didn't even wear a tie at my own wedding!

My practice began to shift when the first-generation iPod Touch was released in September 2007. Even without a speaker, this piece of technology amazed me! All of a sudden my students and I had instant access to a dictionary, thesaurus, and the Google machine wherever we were. Because I allowed my students to use these devices in class, I quickly learned that I needed to change the kinds of questions I asked. Students could search for answers to questions about information, which meant I needed to ask questions that made them think and problem solve.

I'm still asking questions; in fact if you take anything from this book, it is that I do not claim to have all the answers, just a lot of questions. Positive discourse allows me to learn. I appreciate you joining the discussion by reading this book. I know you may have picked up *Block Breaker* because of an interest in *Minecraft*. That's great. But I hope that in it, you will also see a bigger picture—a picture in which tools like *Minecraft* provide opportunities for all kids to feel a level of success and confidence. Good math students are no longer defined by how quickly they can spout correct answers. Good math students are problem solvers and thinkers. In fact, simply using the adjective "good" implies that we have bad math students. I don't believe this at all. All students are math students.

Welcome to what Seymour Papert once described as Mathland: a place where kids can be curious, teachers can give feedback, and everyone can grow together while exploring new ideas and ways of thinking.

<Dream House>

Becoming a Class Full of Block Breakers

One of my grade six students approached me, excitedly. He had figured out a way to "do" math in *Minecraft*.

We were working on a project on designing a "dream house" with a certain amount of square footage for each room. He had made a twenty-minute voiceover video showing off his creation, a mansion that he had made entirely in *Minecraft*. Along the tour, he had signposts explaining his calculations. His work was creative, mathematically sound, and fun.

That year many students learned how to use the power of *Minecraft* to do mathematics. They placed growing patterns, fish tanks, and other structures in their 3-D worlds as a way of answering math problems.

Very memorably, at one point, we tackled a problem about how many people could fit, standing, in a subway car. Students designed the subway car in *Minecraft*, and at one point, there were about fifteen avatars of students in the class working together, crawling all over the subway car, excitedly doing their math work. It truly was inquiry-based learning.

Shortly after this lesson, this class made it on to the local news. The students had a blast telling the reporters about their *Minecraft* creations. In the three-minute television clip titled, "Gaming for Good Grades," the students maturely and persuasively presented themselves and their reasons for working in *Minecraft*.

There is almost unlimited potential when working in a wide open and infinite space like a *Minecraft* world. In this wide open space—and a game based on the inherently mathematical act of laying cubic metre blocks—students can add to their creations and learning as the year goes on.

What if more students learned how to harness *Minecraft*'s potential in service of their mathematical thinking?

Matthew Oldridge, @MatthewOldridge

TEDx speaker, writer, educator

Chapter 1

0 0 0 0 0 0 0 1

Minecraft Meets Civil Rights

If you can't fly then run, if you can't run then walk, if you can't walk then crawl, but whatever you do you have to keep moving forward.
—Martin Luther King, Jr.

I knew it was going to be a very intense meeting. What I didn't know was how that meeting would change my teaching practice forever.

The parents of one of my students had requested to meet with me, the principal, the vice principal, and the resource teacher early in the school year. Their son, one of my grade eight students, was struggling in school. He seemed to have no interest in doing what he was asked to do. Cs and Ds filled his report cards. Worse yet, he wouldn't answer questions about his performance or give any indication of what we could do to help him improve. Frankly, he didn't seem to care.

Granted, he had a pretty different communication style than I or the rest of the school staff did. He had autism and was mainly nonverbal. But his parents had plenty to say about how we needed to change, so their son could show his intelligence.

During the meeting, his father pulled out a piece of paper, stood up, and began to read. "I have a dream," he began, borrowing from Martin Luther King, Jr.'s famous address.

"I have a dream that one day my child will be a functioning member of society. I have a dream that one day my child will hold down a job, be responsible, and be independent. I have a dream that one day my child will have conversations with people like you and I are right now."

It sounded hopeful, until he mentioned what was making these dreams seem impossible: the education system, and by implication, me.

"But until you change something about his school setting, I am afraid that is never going to change."

The Cs and Ds that filled his son's report cards spelled one thing to his parents: that the school thought he was dumb. But to them, we were the ones who didn't understand. This child could take any of his million LEGO pieces and correctly identify which kit they belonged to.

"Please, in his grade eight year, with a progressive administrator and a techy teacher, find a way to unlock the amazing potential we know he has."

Their son was ten months away from heading to high school. His parents wanted to send him there on a successful note. Rightfully so.

It may seem insensitive, but as everyone in the room began to cry, all I could think of was *Minecraft* and block-based coding. And in that moment, the way I viewed teaching and assessment began to change.

You see, for ten years we (the collective school community) had expected this student to live, work, and play in a system that didn't provide much opportunity for his success. Ensuring his compliance (sit still, be quiet, do the worksheet, get good grades) often led to him responding by hitting, which resulted in him being removed from school. Granted, everyone must be a compliant member of society, but as our expectations and methods had the opposite of the desired effect, we clearly needed a different approach.

With permission from his parents, we modified his program to suit his needs in a unique way. If I am being transparent, I felt uncomfortable with this new concept. It meant I had to work hard to be innovative with lessons that could be completed with tools like *Minecraft*. It meant I had to structure time for him differently than for other students. In so many ways, that year challenged me as an educator, and I am forever grateful for it.

All the technology in the world won't make our classrooms "twenty-first-century ready." Redefining our roles as educators will.

#BlockBreaker

Minecraft became this student's portfolio for the rest of the year. The buildings he created showed he had mastered growth patterns in ways he couldn't demonstrate through paper and pencil tasks. And that was only the beginning of the changes we saw.

I was so pleased to see an email from his mom:

> *"Dear Mr. A,*
> *When is the book fair? My son would like to purchase books.*
> *Thanks!"*

I had no idea just how big a deal this request was until they showed up at the book fair. She enthusiastically shared about her son's sudden desire to read. Until then, her son had shown little interest in reading, let alone in buying books. Ten years into his elementary experience, he was finally ready. So off they went, and he purchased three books that day. I'm not sure who was more excited, him or her!

The lesson I learned from that year's *Minecraft* experiment is captured in a famous quote from Ignacio Estrada: **"If a child can't learn the way we teach, we should teach the way they learn."**

Ironically, what I thought was going to be a lot of work resulted in the exact opposite. With his newfound interest in books, for example, I could ask him for summaries, explanations, reflections, and predictions in our English class. He then used *Minecraft* to demonstrate his ability to learn and his understanding of the content. Remember, student product does not always have to be written down. This worked in all of his studies: He built historical settings, recounted wars, designed aquariums, explained patterns, and even built elaborate Rube Goldberg machines.

Changing my teaching methods for this student made me reconsider how I teach and evaluate all of my students. After all, they are all different. The one-size-fits-all methods have never worked.

For the first time in my teaching career, we included *Minecraft* as a required tool in this student's IEP (Individualized Education Plan)—a legal document stating what the goals for this student are and how we plan to achieve the goals. *Minecraft* is a phenomenal educational tool, and one that gets me pretty excited. I'm eager to tell you about how it has helped me teach, and how it can help you too. But it isn't the tool I recommend for every student. That's why this book isn't really about *Minecraft*; it's about personalizing learning and meeting each student's educational needs.

Games change; popularity rises and falls. What I really hope this book does is help you reconsider how we evaluate students' work and how we value students themselves as unique individuals. This student of mine, a young, blond-haired, blue-eyed brilliant teenager, just needed a voice. He successfully completed grade eight and proudly went to high school feeling confident. His secondary teachers have reached out periodically with an update on his progress. Last check he was a B student who was still using his iPad to demonstrate learning with *Minecraft*. Perhaps most importantly, he was no longer getting suspended.

<Lesson>

Minecraft Meets Rube Goldberg

Learning Goal

To demonstrate real-world physics using *Minecraft*.

Minds On

Begin this lesson by asking students a variety of questions, which might include:

1. What do you know about gravity?
2. What happens when you drop an object?
3. Have you ever ridden over a ramp with your bike?
4. How does changing the incline affect your jump?
5. Do you find it more or less difficult to ride down a hill? Why?

Let's Explore

Show students different examples of Rube Goldberg cartoons found on the internet. Ask them to narrate the story happening in each scene. You may also wish to show real Rube Goldberg machines found on YouTube. Explain to students that they are to make a Rube Goldberg machine in *Minecraft*, using the power of redstone, switches, and waterfalls. Encourage students to draw rough diagrams explaining each scene, like the cartoons from earlier. Encourage students to be creative in their thinking and to share ideas with their peers.

Consolidation

This project could run anywhere from a few days to a few weeks, depending on your goals with the activity. On completion, ask students to reflect on the learning goals. Perhaps complete the KWL chart with the group. Have students demonstrate their machines by connecting devices to a projector.

<An Interview with>

Joe Archer (@ArcherJoe)

How have tools like *Minecraft* changed your approach to teaching and learning?

Over the past few years, I have been dabbling and trying out *Minecraft* within the classroom. What I have seen is a new approach to teaching and learning, in that *Minecraft* allows me to provide a visual space for students to represent their understanding and learning in a meaningful, engaging manner that they love and become instantly engaged in. In math especially, it has been fantastic to see their visual representations come to life. Students can now create and demonstrate their learning in a digital/visual manner that shows and explains their work. I am not a fan of tests, so I love that *Minecraft* provides a meaningful way for students to show their understanding. What really convinced me to use *Minecraft* was when an autistic friend who had incredible difficulties sharing his learning was able to demonstrate his knowledge outside of typical performance demonstrations, which were "test-like" in nature for him. Suffice it to say the depth and quality of his work brought tears to my eyes. When I shared his portfolio with his parents, we were all flabbergasted and pleasantly surprised at his A-level work.

What are some of your favourite *Minecraft* tasks?

One of my favourite experiences was when my students created some amazing comparison worlds from Canada's past, focusing on our amazing Native friends, who helped create Canada and develop it to what it is today. Some of the builds were remarkable and innovative in nature; one particular student used redstone to emulate movement in cutting trees down, then transferring the trees through a Conga-type line that eventually led into the construction of an incredible long house, complete with a fire in the hearth!

Another favourite task was exploring various builds that Garrett Zimmerman created with his team for us to see, experience, and explore time periods, eras, and spaces in time and history in which mankind lived, learned, and adapted to environmental conditions. These were incredible virtual field trips that were very similar in nature to actual field trips, with guides and presenters, links, and blackboards sharing the voice of a guide. *Minecraft* has limitless possibilities for today's students, who are less engaged by pen-and-paper tasks from the olden days of teaching. During these virtual field trips, students' educational experiences felt meaningful to them as they explored, innovated, and learned!

WHAT WOULD YOU SAY TO OTHERS HOPING TO GET STARTED WITH *MINECRAFT*?

I was reluctant at first too. My recommendation would be to jump in; take a few online courses on the Microsoft Educator Community, do a few online professional development (PD) sessions, go to workshops presented by *Minecraft* Mentors, watch Skype lessons, etc. Try it out yourself; time will fly by when you begin having fun. And remember that your students are the best sources of information! My students taught me the game, and I constantly go back to my *Minecraft* specialists within the classroom for more learning. When students become the teachers, they feel empowered, and their understanding reaches even higher levels. Even better, through this style of learning and demonstration, they are able to transfer their newfound knowledge to other subject areas.

JOE ARCHER, @ARCHERJOE

Grade 5/6 educator
#MIEFellow #MIEExpert #MIETrainer

Chapter 2

0 0 0 0 0 0 1 0

Why (Math) Education Needs *Minecraft*

If you want to be creative, stay in part a child, with the creativity and invention that characterizes children before they are deformed by adult society.

—Jean Piaget

Researchers are piling loads of money and time into understanding math education: what students need to learn and how they should best learn it. That's a good thing. Math skills are crucial for getting jobs and staying competitive in the economy.

Unfortunately, our education system doesn't do the best job of teaching students about math. I teach in the Canadian province of Ontario. Here, our curriculum divides math into different strands: number sense and numeration, measurement, geometry and spatial sense, patterning and algebra, and data management and probability. But—and this shouldn't surprise any of you reading this—we don't spend an equal amount of time on each strand. Researchers say that, of all the strands, the least amount of time is dedicated to geometry and spatial sense. This is true, despite several studies that suggest most of our math instruction for young children should focus on geometry and spatial sense. Some researchers say that preschool-aged children with good spatial skills do better at math when they are in school, and that their spatial skills are a better indicator of their future math abilities than their early math skills or vocabulary. Some even argue that half of all math education in early years should focus on geometry and measurement.

Paying Attention to Spatial Reasoning

Watch it on the blog: brianaspinall.com/1969-2

The lack of focused attention to building children's spatial sense is a huge problem, because we use spatial sense (sometimes called spatial reasoning) and geometry all the time. Spatial reasoning has three main parts: concepts of space, tools of representation, and processes of reasoning. Simply put, it is the ability to understand where objects are and how they move or exist in a given space. It also includes understanding how those objects fit together, for example, knowing how you can put two triangles together to make a rectangle.

An obvious application of spatial reasoning is sports. It is what enables athletes to know how to chase down soccer balls or change their batting approach so they can drive a baseball into the outfield.

We use spatial reasoning even when working with objects that aren't in motion. Right now, your eyes are moving across these lines of text. You know that all the words fit within the border of the page or screen. Because of that, you know when you need to move to the next page.

It also involves remembering what objects look like. This happens when you read: Your mind remembers the shape of each letter, helping you decipher different words. Spatial reasoning includes being able to picture how an object looks as you make changes to it. In short, it's not just part of math; it's part of every subject. More than that—it's part of every part of life.

We don't need a generation of coders. We need a generation of digital thinkers who might use coding to solve authentic problems. We need problem solvers.

#BlockBreaker

Word problems in math are a way to build students' spatial thinking. They often require students to determine the location of objects based on what they read. And while it can be easy to see how spatial thinking is useful in science, technology, engineering, and mathematics, it's also prominent in the arts. Physical gestures and facial expressions are key parts of communication. Making visual art requires understanding of how different shapes fit together.

It's important to recognize how spatial awareness can—excuse the pun—fit into all subjects. The concepts can seem so abstract that students can quickly become discouraged. Like any set of skills, however, spatial awareness can be learned. It's a skill that can be improved and strengthened. By designing tasks that require students to move and manipulate objects, educators can make these concepts and skills seem relevant and real. Spatial thinking, for example, can be used in a classroom by writing daily schedules in graphs or displaying information in charts. Simply encouraging students to use spatial words such as "left," "right," "up," and "down", especially with unplugged coding activities, instead of relying on vague phrases such as "over there" helps.

One of the most engaging ways to teach spatial reasoning is through games. Games can give students a meaningful way to engage with the subject matter, and they don't have to be a physical activity. Video games require spatial awareness. *Tetris*—which is very similar to *Minecraft*—is one of the most successful games of all time. I have fond memories of playing *Tetris* against my brother on our three-inch-thick gray Gameboys that were connected via a three-foot cable. This was the perfect setup for backseat gaming on long road trips. Today, tools such as *Scratch* allow students to explore geometry while creating *Tetris*-like games.

Minecraft is a great way to incorporate spatial thinking and awareness across subject matters. The basic building block is one cubic metre, but you can change that as you see fit for your students. These digital manipulatives allow students to learn about growing patterns as they make new objects. As students place objects side by side, they strengthen their spatial thinking and awareness. When they build pools and aquariums, they learn about area and volume and how they relate to each other.

Spatial reasoning is only one of the many concepts that can be taught using *Minecraft*. There are clearly applications for math (you'll find even more as you read), but *Minecraft* can also be used to teach other subjects or concepts. Going on scavenger hunts throughout the worlds students have created, for example, teaches them about following directions. And I've already mentioned how I've used this sandbox world to allow students to share their understanding in English, history, and other subjects. That's one of the benefits: The game fits into many subjects, so you can connect concepts and make learning that much more meaningful.

<LESSON>

THE GREAT ESCAPE!

LEARNING GOAL

To create different *Minecraft* mazes and explore experimental probability and sequential instructions

MINDS ON

Ask students whether they have ever done a maze, perhaps on a restaurant placement or in a magazine. Some have probably experienced mazes in different video games. Guide the conversation until you feel confident that all students can define what a maze is.

LET'S EXPLORE

This activity is meant to teach experimental probability, tree diagrams, and organized lists. As a group, flip a few times and tally the results for all to see. Discuss different ways to organize the data and provide an example tree diagram.

Next, ask students whether they could create a maze in *Minecraft* with a specific surface area. The maze should begin with a room containing multiple hallways in which the player of the game has to choose which path to go through. Entering the wrong path would lead to a dead end. Entering the correct path would lead to another room with more hallways. The process would repeat until the student is satisfied with the length of their tunnels.

CONSOLIDATION

Once complete, have students play each other's games and make tree diagrams showing the possible and impossible paths. You may wish to connect a device to a projector and calculate the odds of escaping a certain maze the first time through.

One of the great advantages of using *Minecraft* is most of your students are already familiar with it. There's a good chance they play the game regularly. This benefits everyone in the class. First, it helps you because your students can be the experts and help you teach it. Students learn best when their teachers are confident in what they're teaching. If you're not sure about something, chances are you have a classroom full of people who know the answer. If I have learned anything as a teacher, it is that every student in my class knows something I do not. Second, this helps them because it builds their math skills when they're not in the classroom or doing assignments. Students' math skills often drop during the months when they're not in school. If students spend their time away from the class playing *Minecraft*, there's a chance they'll come to your class ready to learn and maybe to teach you a thing or two.

<GAME>

MINECRAFT + PATTERNING = 3D ALGEBRA WORLD

OBJECTIVE

- Identify and extend patterns.
- Use algebra to describe pattern rules.
- Represent relationships using a table of values.

I cannot take sole credit for this *Minecraft* project. My grade eight student Stephen helped develop this pretty cool "game." Using *Minecraft*, students created and extended block patterns. Players of the game solved each pattern in *Minecraft* before they proceeded to the next pattern.

Each game had a minimum of ten patterns, each more difficult than the previous. Some students added switches that opened doors if the player guessed the correct pattern. Some students created dead ends for players who guessed the pattern incorrectly.

Students collaborated in groups, using words I still don't know. And that is okay; we learned together. I helped with algebraic expressions, and they showed me how *Minecraft* works. During this task, I even had students building *Minecraft* pattern blocks and Facetiming each other from different parts of the school!

Traditionally, students would solve textbook questions by creating a table of values for a pattern. Instead, our students had to first create their own patterns, solve them, and build them. How would you extend this project?

View this activity:

brianaspinall.com/minecraft-patterning-3d-algebra-world

Chapter 3

0 0 0 0 0 0 1 1

The Father of Modern Computing

We can only see a short distance ahead, but we can see plenty there that needs to be done.
—Alan Turing

When I first had the idea to write a sequel to *Code Breaker*, I wanted to be certain the message was clear: Tools will change. Technology will change. Our approaches to teaching and learning should too, not to reflect these new tools, but to reflect the ways in which our young people learn, interact and live. It is imperative to meet them where they are, move them forward and never give up on them. Today millions of young people enjoy creating content with *Minecraft*, but tomorrow they may be playing a different game or using a new technology. What must remain constant is our commitment to providing opportunities for students to explore, be curious, and create solutions to authentic problems.

I knew I wanted to write something with the word "Breaker" in the title. A bit of a brand strategy that carries a multifold meaning of being discontented with the status quo, the notion of challenging beliefs and systems, and my desire to engage in positive discourse to make educational changes to better ourselves and our young people.

Alan Turing, often referred to as the father of modern computing, was a brilliant mathematician who researched computer science and artificial intelligence during the Second World War. While working for the Government Code and Cypher School at Bletchley Park, Britain's code-breaking centre, Turing played a very important role in intercepting and cracking coded messages, thus enabling allies to defeat the Nazis on more than one occasion. Many people believe that Turing alone shortened the war by up to two years.

When I read about integrating coding into school lessons, I worry that it will become part of the curriculum. I fear that a coding curriculum would create a level of standardization based on a quantity of correctness—which contradicts the notion of creativity inherent in coding. We all know that the second coding becomes a curriculum, we will have to grade it. It doesn't matter what the activity is; as soon as reporting becomes mandatory, the fun gets sucked right out of it. That said, I'm all for coding in school, clearly, as long as we approach it as a tool for learning to solve authentic problems, much like Alan Turing did. With this amazing tool, we can harness the critical thinking, creativity, and brilliant ideas our young people have.

"You do not inspire people by showing them how powerful you are. You inspire people by showing them how powerful they are." —Alexander Den Heijer

#BlockBreaker

<LESSON>

CHANGING THE LOAD

LEARNING GOAL

To discover how surface area relates to volume of rectangular prisms

MINDS ON

Provide students with various household containers such as cereal boxes. Ask them to measure the length, width, and height of each box to determine its surface area and volume.

In this activity, students are asked to create different arrangements of boxes that are to be loaded onto a flatbed. With *Minecraft*, we can have students first create the trucks to scale for the different loads. This might be a great way to engage parents or community members. Imagine measuring the size of a flatbed truck in the school parking lot!

LET'S EXPLORE

Tell students that the moving company WEMOVE needs their help in finding the most efficient way to stack boxes on their flatbed trucks. Provide students with pictures of different trucks and ask them to research possible truck dimensions. Tell students they are to create the trucks in *Minecraft* first and then rearrange a set number of boxes to fit accordingly. You may scaffold the number of boxes for each learner. Ask students to take screen shots as they rearrange their boxes, so they can explain their thinking each time.

CONSOLIDATION

Have students present their trucks and arranged boxes, justifying why they think theirs is the most efficient. Ask them to explain, using their math vocabulary. Opportunities for assessment include observation, conversation, student product, and their demonstration.

I hope my point is clear. Math (like coding and all creative learning) is not something we can score like golf. I am fearful that our approaches to coding could become binary—right or wrong. The reality is, as Seymour Papert writes in *Mindstorms,* you almost never get the program right the first time you code it. When student work is seen as fixable, rather than right or wrong, we imply growth.

This mindset challenges us to redefine what it means to fail at school.

Whether you are breaking blocks or breaking codes, consider what it is we want from our students. Both of these examples are sandbox spaces with no correct answer. Instead, in *Minecraft* and in coding, students develop games, test simulators, engage with robotics, ask questions, make observations, change variables, and learn from reflecting on experiences. In a world that demands creativity and problem solving, being right all the time just isn't possible. Nor is it desirable. What is desirable is hearing students ask, "What would happen if I tried this?" instead of "What grade did I get?"

When student work is seen as fixable, rather than right or wrong, we imply growth. This mindset challenges us to redefine what it means to fail at school.

#BlockBreaker

I recently attended a workshop with high school teachers who were exploring a gradeless approach. The idea is simple: You can still mark work and record it, but you don't have to put a grade on student work. The reality is that no matter how much feedback you give on your students' work, if you attach a grade to it, your students aren't going to pay attention to the feedback. They will see only the grade. And grades imply an endpoint.

Done.

Finished.

Tossed in the trash bin.

I remember playing the game of school in both high school and university. In high school, I would intentionally select courses I knew I could ace in the same semester as more difficult ones so that I could maintain a specific average. After all, my average was all that mattered to get into university. I would study less, knowing that an exam score worth twenty percent would hardly impact my mark, as long as it was in the nineties. Worst-case scenario, I would end up with a seventy-five. My university experience was no different. Once I had a course syllabus on day one, I would mathematically strategize which assignments I needed to put more effort into in order to pass the class or get an A. Getting the grade was more important to me than learning the material. Just tell me what you want me to do, and I will go do it. If I don't, I will be placed on academic probation for failing to maintain a standard. Let the math games begin!

Note:

The next section of the book began as a blog post that struck a nerve. If you want to read the original post and the ensuing comments, go to brianaspinall.com/that-age-old-battle-please-remove-your-hat-in-school.

Rules, Requirements, and Other Things That Prevent Real Learning

Hats (specifically removing them in the building) was a recurring topic of conversation in my school for a number of years. Until recently, enforcing this rule was a constant battle that many teachers jumped into every morning. They'd stand guard at the door and sternly call out "Hats, please!" instead of greeting students with a far more pleasant, "Good morning!" Nope, "Hats, please!" were the words that set the tone for the day—and not in a good way.

After enough years of this battle, we finally asked, why do we ask students to remove hats when they enter the school? When we discussed the rule as a staff, we determined a few reasons:

- It is a sign of respect.
- Men always took hats off indoors in the 19xxs.

That is about as far as we got. With the respect piece aside, we focused on this being perhaps a twentieth-century rule. Men no longer remove hats at the mall, the gas station, the hardware store, etc. And what about women? Women wear hats too.

About ten minutes into an internet search on the question, I noticed a pattern regarding safety. There were comments about identifying students on camera. There were comments about hiding weapons in hats. Of course there also were many comments about the politeness of removing a hat indoors but not just at school—anywhere indoors.

Ultimately, we decided to stop enforcing this rule at our school, and the hats seemed to come off anyway. Maybe not as soon as students entered the building but certainly at their lockers. This made me think about some of the other rules and requirements that affect school culture simply because they are mandated. What about, for example, the "gum rule?" If we stopped shouting, "Gum, please!" will they stop sticking it to desks and keyboards? Might this apply to food and drinks? If we stopped letting the bells dictate learning and allowed kids to eat when they are hungry, how might learning change?

And if we stopped giving homework or grades? How might that improve the way we teach and assess students?

So much of what we do in schools harkens back to the old, authoritarian way of running schools. If we want to prepare our students for life in the real world, perhaps it's time to ditch some of the rules and requirements that distract from real learning.

Chapter 4

0 0 0 0 0 1 0 0

STEM Circuits with Redstone

The biggest risk is not taking any risk. In a world that is changing really quickly, the only strategy that is guaranteed to fail is not taking risks.

—Mark Zuckerberg

I promised myself I was not going to write a "how to *Minecraft*" book but instead would focus on teaching practices, pedagogy, and thought leadership. I could not have put this book together, however, without discussing redstone. In *Minecraft*, players obtain redstone through a variety of methods. It dawned on me a few years ago that I could discuss financial literacy with my class if we viewed redstone as a currency. After all, you find it, mine it, save it, and store it. You use it to build electrical circuits and switches that control power in the game.

<LESSON>

EIGHT-BIT ART

LEARNING GOAL

To increase understanding of proportional relationships by enlarging artwork in *Minecraft*

MINDS ON

Ask students whether they have ever played Battleship or a similar game that uses a grid system. Encourage students to look for grids within the classroom.

Show different examples of maps and discuss the scaling of each one. How big is one centimetre on this map?

Provide students with different examples of eight-bit art found online.

LET'S EXPLORE

Challenge students to recreate the art in 3D inside *Minecraft* to a specific scale. Have them build a backend and ask what it might look like if you could transform flat art to 3D.

CONSOLIDATION

Have students take turns presenting their scaled art to the class while discussing the scale unit each time. Have students explain what they think the back side would look like and have them show this to the class in *Minecraft*.

POSSIBLE EXTENSION

Students could take measurements of the school (or classroom) and build it to scale in *Minecraft*. You may wish to assign certain buildings from your town to certain students to build your entire community to scale.

I can't stress enough: This chapter is not about just redstone but rather the idea of spiraling curriculum, teaching beyond the silo of single expectations. Spiraling curriculum is what we do when we revisit topics over time, gradually increasing the complexity of the learning task. Our best approach to teaching and learning is quite often covering multiple expectations in one task. While playing with *Minecraft* in math class is awesome, talking about electrical circuits, learning from trial and error, and discussing financial literacy is even more awesomer! (My spellcheck is not underlining awesomer, so the word stays!) Some of the best Rube Goldberg machines I have seen exist in *Minecraft*.

Minecraft offers an endless canvas where students can stretch ideas beyond their imaginations. When you have students simultaneously build physical structures in the physical space as well as digital structures in the digital space, then they can make connections and comparisons, explore options, and ask, "What if I tried this?"

We have always been able to ask "What if?" in schools. What has changed in the past decade or so is technology. When implemented properly and used for learning, technology allows us to explore many possible solutions to the "what if" question. In most of life, there isn't just one correct answer or a single solution. Multiple options are viable, and in a perfect guided-inquiry task, the teacher may not even know what the solution is. As such, failure means something completely different than receiving 49 percent on an exam.

Kids might forget dates and formulas, but they will never forget who you are as a person.

#BlockBreaker

Lastly, regarding redstone and *Minecraft* in general, our young people are creating so much content for YouTube that we have an opportunity to engage in conversations about their ideas. Note that most of the time, our students are making said content on their own time. In many ways, this is what a flipped classroom looks like. As a teacher of grades seven and eight, I have a media curriculum to cover and an oral communication curriculum to cover. It just makes sense to me to use the student products kids are developing outside of the classroom during in-class discussions. I realize I have gone down a bit of a rabbit hole here, but I have struck a personal chord with the notion of covering curriculum.

The word *cover* has a few meanings. To some it means dealing with a subject by describing the most important criteria. I like this. A lot. But the word *cover* can also mean to conceal or hide. Early in my teaching career, I was guilty of reminding my students about all the curriculum we had to cover in a very short period. I would stand at the front, acting like a delivery person who was distributing curriculum. We had a saying at my former school:

It is okay to be where you are.

It is *not* okay to stay there.

A good reminder that we got into this business as lifelong learners. Back to me at the front delivering curriculum: That is where I was in my practice. I have grown over time and through reflecting on experience. I no longer cover curriculum but prefer to have students *uncover* curriculum through authentic tasks. And some tasks would definitely include redstone.

The Real 1:1 Is Not about Devices

As I reflect on the way my classroom practices have changed in the past few years, I realize just how little I consider technology. I use it, of course, but I don't think about using it nearly as much as I did early on. Technology is simply embedded into my practice. It feels like a natural fit now, but it took time and energy to get there—two things teachers don't have much of during the week. Between raising families, coaching sports teams, and planning lessons and marking at night (forget having a social life), learning about new tools and technologies can be challenging. Trying a new app with a full class of kids generates a lot of anxiety and fear. We wonder, what happens if the technology fails? (And, like student work, is the technology fixable? How do we define "failure?")

But time and energy, though real obstacles, are excuses we have to overcome. If we worked in industry or medicine and didn't keep up with best practices, we would be fired. That's a scary thought. Integrating technology into our lessons is a non-negotiable. We are far enough into the future that technology is a must. The question isn't whether to use it, but how? Which tools best serve our purposes of providing personalized learning, making meaningful content connections, and helping students find their passions?

Instead of focusing on technology or a specific tool, let's focus on our pedagogy. How do you plan to implement something like genius hour? Is giving every kid an iDevice and telling them to all complete the same task any better than not using the iDevice at all? Using the latest app simply for the sake of being able to say you are using the latest app seems backwards. Green screens are fun, but what are we truly learning in the process? Let's talk about that in class instead of who made the coolest video.

Although there is no app for great teaching, the proper implementation of technology has the power to make all kids successful. Yes—all! But making all kids successful puts a tremendous onus on them to want to learn. This process takes time. We need to move away from structured charts and rubrics that seem to baby-step kids through tasks and focus instead on big ideas, inquiry, and student passions. Sure, many kids need the scaffolding, but the one-size-fits-all model of schooling is not acceptable. If our goal is to truly personalize learning, differentiate instruction, and scaffold lessons, every student's program is unique. Technology allows this to happen, but it won't happen overnight, and this throws a giant monkey wrench into current methods of assessment and evaluation where there is a grade-level standard. What about those kids above grade level? They need as much attention as those "below" grade level "standards."

Since school began, we have always focused on student weaknesses and next steps. "Little Johnny excels in math but needs help reading, so let's focus on that." I highly doubt little Johnny is going to pursue a career in reading. Don't get me wrong. I am not suggesting we ignore the gaps in little Johnny's learning; I'm just suggesting that we have tools and technologies to assist little Johnny with his reading—now can he go change the world *with* math? There is a reason I studied computer science at university, and it wasn't because I loved to read and write.

Chapter 5

0 0 0 0 0 1 0 1

How to Think about Computational Thinking

What counts in a classroom is not what the teacher teaches; it's what the learner learns.

—Alfie Kohn

When people talk about video games in general (and *Minecraft* would definitely fit into this category), you wouldn't be alone if you pictured pale-skinned computer whizzes spending their lives sitting on couches in their parents' basements, one hand on a joystick, the other in a bag of potato chips. That might have been true for some people of our generation, but we are not teaching us; we are teaching today's generation of kids. This generation has grown up immersed in computer technology.

Everyone uses it. It's a regular part of society and social interaction.

Why stress this point? Because many educators—myself included—like to talk about "computational thinking." We often talk about computational thinking when we talk about computer science or the importance of teaching kids to code. This means many people—understandably so—assume that computational thinking and computer science are the same thing. And that makes non-techy educators nervous. They think that because they're not specialists in computer science, they can't model computational thinking for their students.

I'm a big fan of teaching students to code, and I have a background in computer science. I love it! Therefore, let me say with some passion and authority, computational thinking and computer science are not the same thing. Everyone uses computational thinking, so anyone can learn to teach and model it.

The standard misconception is that computational thinking means thinking like a computer. The truth is that it is more about thinking like a computer scientist. And a designer. And an artist. When faced with open-ended problems, we must determine plausible solutions based on empathy, audience needs, and short- and long-term goals. Most of the time, these problems involve some sort of technology, but considering what we do with it, how we use it, and how we manipulate it is when innovation occurs. And that's where computational thinking comes in.

What is Computational Thinking?

View the blog:
brianaspinall.com/what-is-computational-thinking

Computers don't—and can't—think (with the exception of research in artificial intelligence [AI], but even that is artificial—this was perhaps the best CS joke EVER). Computers just follow directions. Those directions ultimately come from people. "Computational" describes a kind of thinking that focuses on identifying problems and designing systems to solve them. Computational thinking asks two main questions: What problems are we trying to solve? What's the best way to solve these problems?

Computational thinking involves . . .

- breaking a problem down into smaller, manageable parts (decomposition)
- recognizing patterns
- focusing on relevant, important information and ignoring irrelevant information (abstraction)
- creating step-by-step solutions to solve problems (algorithms)

That may sound complicated, but those are all things you do all day, every day. Take the decision to put on a raincoat when it's raining. You know you need to wear clothes that are appropriate to the weather. You break that down into what specific things you need to wear: what coat, what shirt, what pants, what shoes, and so on. You recognize patterns. You know, for example, that a down-filled parka isn't going to be helpful during a rainstorm. Neither is a light shawl. You then focus on the coats you have that will be helpful. You don't try on a parka because you know you won't need it. After that, you put on your raincoat.

How many computers were involved in that decision?

None.

You simply used logical reasoning to find a solution—a strategy used in computational thinking.

Coding is a final step of computational thinking. Can you code an algorithm to help solve the problem? Can you write it in words first?

What is the procedure for making toast? There's even some coding in *Minecraft*. However, the steps you need to take to build and change things are the same. Computational thinking is seeing problems and developing solutions for them rather than simply finding answers. How do you check your math work? Just ask BOB (back of book, just before the glossary; all the textbook answers at our fingertips).

As Jeannette Wing wrote in 2006, when she helped further generalize the term *computational thinking*, computational thinking is part of every area of life. "Computational thinking will be a reality when it is so integral to human endeavours it disappears as an explicit philosophy."

10 Reasons Kids Should Code

View the blog:
brianaspinall.com/10-reasons-kids-should-learn-to-code

The thing is, computational thinking already is a part of every human endeavour, whether we realize it or not. As educators, it's our job to make sure our students can think this way. After all, an initial step in the design thinking process is about empathizing with those struggling with the problem we are trying to solve, something computers are unable to comprehend but definitely something we need to discuss in this day and age. With so much school violence, so many political agendas and social media posts, it is imperative that we model empathy and teach students to be empathetic toward others.

<An Interview with>

Steve Isaacs (@mr_isaacs)

How have tools like *Minecraft* changed your approach to teaching and learning?

Minecraft truly taught me to step back and let the students drive the learning. I learned quickly about how we learn in informal learning spaces, in nontraditional ways, through this game. All game tutorials and resources are community generated (wikis, YouTube videos, etc.) and have demonstrated to me how we can truly apply on-demand learning in an authentic way. This led me to be much more open-ended in my "teaching" and move more toward teaching general concepts and guiding the process.

The learning in my class revolves around iterative design. I can teach the iterative design process but don't have to be responsible for teaching kids how to do everything in *Minecraft*. They are the experts. I learned to embrace that. Taking on the role of co-learner in the classroom became a joy for me. Some students took leadership roles, which ranged from creating and managing the class *Minecraft* server to defining their own roles within a team to leverage their strengths and support their peers.

Other changes that occurred in my classroom came with the realization that my students needed to be part of the constructivist learning environment and give back to the community by creating resources (step-by-step tutorials, videos, etc.) to share their knowledge and teach others. Their resources became amazing assessment tools. After all, if we can teach others how to do something concisely, we are certainly demonstrating our own understanding. To me, this was transformational in terms of authentic learning and assessment.

What are some of your favourite *Minecraft* tasks?

Since I teach game design and development, automation in *Minecraft* (redstone, command blocking, coding, etc.) is what I am most excited about. It's important to automate functions in a game, and *Minecraft* provides amazing opportunities for students to automate. When students use their knowledge and problem-solving skills, they experience aha moments as they automate within the game. These are the same ideas that make coding so profound as a tool for learning. Students discover that there are many ways to solve a problem. They are empowered when they make a discovery and can then share that idea with the rest of the class (and my other classes). I love to share my students' learning with others (and celebrate their accomplishments) when they figure out new solutions.

What would you say to others hoping to get started with *Minecraft*?

I think Nike said it best: Just do it! Actually, I encourage anyone new to engage with the amazing community of *Minecraft* educators. The #MINECRAFTEDU hashtag is widely used, and there are so many passionate educators who love to help teachers get started. There's a Tuesday night (8:00 pm ET) #minecraftedu Twitter chat that I highly recommend. Also, the education.minecraft.net site is the hub for the *Minecraft* education edition, and it hosts a discussion area, huge lesson plan repository of lessons contributed by educators, and a directory of global *Minecraft* mentors.

Finally, and probably most importantly, leverage student expertise. Students love to teach teachers how to play *Minecraft*. Learn with and from your students! It's so empowering for students to teach, and your willingness to learn from them demonstrates that we are all learners.

What is Minefaire?

Minefaire is a massive *Minecraft* fan experience. We are the only official community event in North America, and we hold the Guinness World Record for the most attendees at an event for a single video game, with over 17,000 attendees at our Los Angeles event in April 2018. The event celebrates everything *Minecraft* while bringing the community together. Big name YouTubers are at all of the events for meet-and-greets with their fans, and they participate in activities on our stages. There are four stages total, including our Diamond Stage, which is home to many of the sessions, including YouTubers, as well as our costume contest. Our Build Battle Stage provides attendees with opportunities to participate in guild battles on stage against other attendees and our rising YouTube stars. Our Inspiration Stage is home to twenty-minute presentations throughout the day showcasing great things people are doing with *Minecraft*. Finally, our Learning Lab hosts hands-on workshops throughout the day where attendees learn everything from how to create minigames to how to change behaviours of "mobs" with behaviour packs.

In addition to our stages, we have a virtual reality (VR) area with forty after-mixed reality headsets, where attendees get to experience *Minecraft* in VR. We also have a variety of vendors at the events and several large gaming arenas run by server partners such as Mineplex, and Feed the Beast, where attendees can compete in tournament-style mini-game play.

STEVEN ISAACS, @MR_ISAACS

educator, video game development
ISTE2016 Outstanding Teacher
Minecraft mentor and @Minefaire producer

Chapter 6

0 0 0 0 0 1 1 0

How Can We Assess Creativity?

The greatest sign of success for a teacher . . . is to be able to say, "The children are now working as if I did not exist."
—Maria Montessori

I've always said I learn more from my students than they learn from me.

As you may have noticed, I have a lot of concerns with traditional assessment methods. Let me rephrase that. Assessment for learning and as learning are important for student growth. Assessment of learning (evaluation) doesn't much help students learn and grow. It is meant to communicate learning at the end of a cycle to parents and other teachers. The primary purpose of assessment and evaluation is to improve student learning, but I do not believe that standardized testing and marking practices are effective in determining what people really know. Grades are for stakeholders, not learners. Feedback is for the learner.

Grades have their place and serve their purpose, but I believe they would be higher at the end of the year if we stopped putting them on everything students do during the learning cycle. Grades are quantitative measures of student learning at the end of a learning cycle, not during. But I'm not the only one who shares this frustration. My students do too.

They're also the ones who showed me about how our faulty evaluation practices extend even into the subjects we consider more creative. A few years ago, we hosted a youth talk, modeled after the TEDx events. We wanted to give students in the intermediate grades (middle school) a chance to share their thoughts on a stage in front of all stakeholders.

One student in grade seven presented a talk about his experiences with genius hour. He described how he struggled in art class, but he loved genius hour. During genius hour, he could draw and doodle whatever he wanted. But his art class was different. In art class, he was told what he had to create. Then all the students' work was ranked accordingly.

He found that frustrating.

"How can you evaluate my creativity?" he asked.

Good question.

He certainly had a point. If we tell students what to create in art class, how are we teaching them to be creative?

Granted, there is a time and place for showing students good pieces of art and asking them to create their own. They can provide examples of spatial reasoning and thinking. But when teachers hold up certain students' work as "best," it can discourage others from creating their own. That's how this student felt: discouraged. And slightly confused. The art class was telling him what creativity should look like.

<MEMORY>

The Value of Student Choice

When I was in grade ten, Mrs. Boudreau took a chance on me. If you have seen me speak, you might be familiar with this story, as it means a great deal to me and I share it regularly. In my Media Studies class, we were given the task of researching a celebrity, organizing specific information, and presenting it back. Not being a fan of cut-and-paste activities, I immediately jumped at the chance to build a website. As I mentioned in *Code Breaker*, my dad was a self-employed mortgage broker at the time, learning HTML to create a digital footprint for himself beyond the yellow pages of the phone book. I had been following his actions and felt empowered to write code to put things on a computer screen. I pitched the idea to Mrs. Boudreau, and she allowed me to build a 2pac fan page. As teachers do, she began bragging about her students' work in the staff room, and people began to take notice, leading me to monetise my web-building skills and portfolio before graduating from high school in the late nineties.

As you will see in this surprise reunion video with Mrs. Boudreau, themes such as genius hour can be the catalyst for change. I was given a choice in high school that forever changed my path in life, and I hope to provide the same opportunities for my students.

Being reunited with a former teacher of mine will forever be one of my fondest moments.

I hope students feel the same way when we cross paths in the future. Sometimes it's the simplest decisions we make that can have the greatest impact—both positively and negatively. Just be mindful.

Thank you, Mrs. Boudreau.

View the blog:

brianaspinall.com/the-value-of-student-choice

The assessments were taking the creativity out of art, even if the class claimed to do otherwise.

This contradictory thinking can be found throughout our discussions of educational reform. We spend a lot of time throwing around phrases such as "twenty-first-century pedagogy" and "passion projects." Here's my current passion project: Let's ditch these discussions and focus our energy on changing how we evaluate students. What's the point of using an innovative teaching method if we're marking students the same way we did years ago?

There is a place for play and creativity in the classroom. Personally, I have a problem with timetables and scheduled time slots for different subjects. It's hard for me to tell students when they can learn and when they can't, when they can eat and when they can't. We often have working lunches in my class. I understand there are practical constraints that make these conventions necessary. I'll live with scheduled lunchtimes, for now.

Who a teacher is will always outweigh what a teacher teaches. Relationships matter.

#BlockBreaker

If we are truly going to change education, we have to do more than change the physical aspects of our schools. In recent years, many schools have removed their computer labs. I've heard of schools doing this because they want to get away from having students sitting in uniform rows while they all work on the same assignments. Having students all complete the same tasks on computers is the same, people say, as having them all do the same problems in workbooks. Instead of computer labs, they say, we need to give students tablets and other mobile devices. But if a class set of tablets is used in the same manner as those clunky desktops in the computer lab, nothing meaningful has changed.

The Power of Math Visualization

View the blog:
brianaspinall.com/the-power-of-math-visualization

We can't just change the tools we use to teach. We must change the way we teach.

I believe that *Minecraft* is an excellent tool to teach students spatial reasoning, computational thinking, and design thinking. I also believe humans can learn more by playing and experimenting than by listening to a lecture. I beg you, however: Don't consider introducing *Minecraft* into your teaching if you're just going to compare what students make against each other. If students are being judged based on each other's work, you're not teaching in a new way.

Genius Hour—Looking Back to Move Forward

Genius hour, a "progressive" approach to teaching and learning, has found its place in classrooms across the globe. The notion of encouraging kids to learn through play, however, has been around forever. Jean Piaget was a pioneer in researching how kids learn. His theory of constructivism suggests that kids learn by doing and making connections. That is, kids learn by making mental and physical models of the world around them. Seymour Papert, who is often regarded as the godfather of educational technology, was a bit of a disruptor who made bold claims against decisions at the school level. From what I have read about him, it appears he was never fond of computer labs and pointed out that "we don't teach kids about pencils at the pencil lab." Like him, I want the computer to be seen and used as a tool for learning, not simply for typing, as it once was in many cases when the computer lab was new.

After World War II, villages in Reggio Emilia, Italy, decided their kids should learn through play-based approaches at very young ages. With the help of psychologist Loris Malaguzzi, the Reggio Emilia approach was founded on these principles:

- Children must have some control over the direction of their learning.
- Children must be able to learn through experiences of touching, moving, listening, and observing.
- Children have a relationship with other children and with material items in the world that they must be allowed to explore.
- Children must have endless ways and opportunities to express themselves.

I love the work being shared regarding genius hour and passion projects. My concern is that schools too often limit these times of inquiry and innovation to scheduled activities based on a structured week made up of isolated subjects and strands because of systematic policies, procedures, and regulations. I understand the hesitation to make genius hour an all-day thing. After all, evaluating student-centred learning approaches can be very challenging in the era of standardization. Fortunately, we have the Teachers Throwing Out Grades (#ttog) movement and countless innovative educators moving the ship forward.

Looking forward, I am confident that new technologies (such as *Minecraft*) will continue to shift pedagogy to a place those before us dreamed about. With tools such as *Minecraft*, we can create things like Seymour Papert's Mathland.

Chapter 7

0 0 1 1 0 1 1 1

Hard Work and the Importance of Play

We do not learn from experience . . . .
We learn from reflecting on experience.
—John Dewey

"**All we do is play** in Mr. A's class."

Boy, have I heard this a lot. Somehow, somewhere along the continuum of school, play got relegated to the younger grades. In older grades, play is seen as negative—a waste of time. But, as Mr. Rogers said, play is the work of the child. And there is that other word: *work*. Has school really become a binary system in which we either work or play? I for one think the notion of "work" carries with it a statement of discomfort.

Cutting the grass sounds like work. Cleaning the gutters sounds like work. I certainly do not enjoy either of those activities.

Play, on the other hand, sounds like fun. It also helps to facilitate the creative thinking process through inquiry and discovery. Sure, some will argue work can do the same, but I think the level of enjoyment would differ. If we are being honest, if we enjoy work, do we see it as work or play?

Evaluating creativity may be impossible—and as my student pointed out, contradictory.

But we can, and should, make our classrooms places that foster creativity.

We might think we're heading to a science-fiction universe by teaching students to code or build robotics. Given the many ways robotics and AI are used today, maybe we are. But I'd like us to consider incorporating tools such as *Minecraft* into the classroom as an invitation to time travel into our past—our childhood. It's really an invitation to play.

Tech Trends and Defining Failure

View the blog:
brianaspinall.com/tech-trends-defining-failure

Educators are adopting methods that emphasize student choice and project-based learning. Much of this is owed to Jean Piaget and his constructivist approach to teaching and learning. His main point was that children learn best when they are doing something or making something. Piaget expressed his ideas in his developmental stage theory. Basically, Piaget argued that children learn things in different stages. They need play to help them learn. Appropriate play can help children learn new things and incorporate what they're learning into what they already know and do. Piaget taught that play is especially important when children are learning languages, but it can be applied to any skill children are learning.

As children progress through the developmental stages, their play becomes more imaginative. They take what they're doing when they play and apply it to the things they do when they're not playing. Play is important, Piaget argued, because it helps students make life decisions.

Some educators have developed entire teaching systems—and in some cases, schools—on Piaget's ideas. Take the Reggio-Emilia approach, developed by psychologist Loris Malaguzzi and named for the Italian villages where this idea took off after World War II. This method stresses that children need some control over how and what they learn. Children best learn through exploration and involving their senses: moving, tasting, touching. This is why it's important to have children do projects. It reinforces their learning.

Often, teachers determine what projects students should do based on what students are already doing. They observe what their students' interests are and assign projects based on those interests. Students have an active role in their learning: They are like apprentices or researchers. Students work on projects that are about real-life problems and situations.

But while children direct their learning, they do not do it alone. Children in these classrooms learn as members of a community. Parents are also involved with how things work in Reggio-Emilia schools: They volunteer and give feedback about curriculum. That's a key part of the Reggio-Emilia method. It's not enough for students to just be doing real-life activities. They need to do it together, as part of a team. They get feedback from each other and modify their actions as a result of what others say.

It might not be possible to implement all of these ideas at a school-wide or district-wide level, but we can start as individual teachers in our classrooms. We could begin by making our classes look a lot more like kindergarten.

Encouraging students to take risks forces us to redefine what it means to fail at school.

#BlockBreaker

That's what Mitch Resnick thinks. Resnick heads up the Lifelong Kindergarten group at the MIT Media Lab. You are likely familiar with Resnick's work. His team developed *Scratch,* the block coding program that has introduced so many to coding, and he's worked with LEGO on their Mindstorms robotics kits. He thinks robots and digital tools, when used properly, are similar to the blocks or finger paint used in kindergarten: They are the tools that help children learn.

Like many people, Resnick says what students need more and more in a rapidly changing information environment is the ability to apply what they're learning. Knowledge abounds, so students don't need to learn more—they need to learn how to apply that knowledge.

Digital technologies can offer that kind of experience, Resnick says, but it has to be done well. "Most schools," he wrote in 2013, "use digital technologies simply to extend and reinforce the information-delivery approach, using computers to deliver information just as they use lectures and books." Digital technologies on their own do not make teaching innovative or create a "kindergarten-like" atmosphere, but they should be designed and used to support students' creativity and play.

Minecraft is a digital resource that does make our classrooms seem more like kindergarten. It requires students to build and create and to explore situations from a variety of perspectives. Students can work together. They give each other feedback and change their plans as a result. If we want to encourage our students to learn and develop through play, *Minecraft* is a great place to start. Sure, we have always done this with linking cubes and other math manipulatives, but the infinite canvas *Minecraft* offers, as well as no clean up, makes for a great supplement.

View this activity:

brianaspinall.com/
3-ways-to-engage-students-with-hard-fun

Three Ways to Engage Students with Hard Fun

Student voice and choice are crucial for learning. When something makes sense to us, it sticks in our minds. Getting that content to stick requires students to have experience with the content being taught. When students have endless ways to demonstrate learning, they are empowered to seek more, do more, and create more. Student choice provides a level of equity. Often though, choices are too vague for students to decide a course of action or direction. In my mind, plopping students in sandbox tools such as *Scratch* or *Minecraft* allows for a great integration of both choice and voice, while allowing the teacher to provide some direction. Asking students to program a Mother's Day greeting card, for example, provides many opportunities for students to make choices while still following specific instructions. Student choice doesn't always have to mean "whatever you want" but instead can mean "whatever you want within these parameters." Too much choice only creates problems for students (and adults) who are unable to filter through options independently without a prior schema of the activities. After all, we don't learn from experience; we learn from reflection on experiences.

1. Unplugged Coding

Have you seen the printable code blocks from *Scratch Jr.* and *Scratch*? These transparent images are perfect manipulatives to have students write scripts on an interactive whiteboard (IWB). Classmates can follow along from their seats, try the script, and provide feedback to the students at the front. Other options include creating scripts that contain bugs, projecting them to the interactive whiteboard, and having students try to debug in real time. Immediate feedback from the environment intrinsically motivates students to want to solve the puzzle. Like games that are both challenging and are rewarding, experience is an example of "hard fun."

2. Green Screen Public Service Announcements

Perhaps you are studying body image or bullying in health class. By combining green screens apps with the IWB, students can seamlessly and quickly swap backgrounds to add different scenes. While the task might be to create a public service announcement (PSA) to inform younger students about an issue, having to make choices about the scene, tool, background, and content engages students and makes them invest in their learning. A by-product of the process of making a piece of media is exploring the tools to carry it out. Students would engage in "hard fun" while demonstrating other twenty-first-century competencies such as creativity, collaboration, problem solving, and organization.

3. Making with *Minecraft*

Minecraft. Need I say more? I love having students create structures in *Minecraft* that represent scenes from stories they are writing about. By providing students an opportunity to orally tell a story while navigating a *Minecraft* town they have created, word choice improves. I have had students use *Minecraft* to organize ideas, develop characters, and bring ideas to life before the writing process.

One way to improve writing and communication is to encourage students to write adjectives to describe what they see and what they have built in the game. A bat becomes a "scary bat" when they see it in *Minecraft*. In my class, we love connecting our tablets to the projector to share our creations on our IWB because it allows everyone to see, share, and be involved in the design thinking process. Perhaps most importantly, the ability to annotate over a *Minecraft* visual is powerful!

Chapter 8

0 0 1 1 1 0 0 0

Hard Fun

Decide in your heart of hearts
what really excites and challenges you,
and start moving your life in that direction.
—Chris Hadfield

Seymour Papert was way ahead of his time with his thinking. In fact, it is quite common for me to articulate a simple idea only to find that he has written a research paper on the very subject. A brilliant man. He was also a mathematician who co-developed LOGO, the first block-based coding language in the late 1960s to engage students with mathematics. In fact, Mitch Resnick and his team built *Scratch* based on LOGO.

5 Stages of the Design Thinking Process

1. **Empathize**: Gain an understanding of your audience and the problem to be solved.

2. **Define**: Once data have been collected, clear goals should be established.

3. **Ideate**: Team members actively work together to generate a list of possible outcomes and solutions.

4. **Prototype**: Members of the team will begin to make ideas tangible by building models to test.

5. **Test**: Finally, prototype will be put to the test to ensure that goals have been met.

Five Stages of the Design Thinking Process

View the blog:
brianaspinall.com/
5-stages-of-the-design-thinking-process

Having read countless websites, articles, and research papers written by Papert or even about him, the notion of "hard fun" continues to pop up. Over and over again, the message is that if we enjoy what we are doing, we work better and learn more. The best fun is hard fun done while working.

You might argue that this idea is very simple. In fact, it probably is. But when you consider the feeling you get when hard work pays off, it makes a great deal of sense. Games are hard fun. Puzzles are hard fun. Writing two books was super hard fun for me! When my grandfather was diagnosed with Alzheimer's Disease, the doctor prescribed a Nintendo DS and the game Brain Age. It turns out that hard fun isn't just fun; it's good for you!

Incorporating hard fun into learning experiences forces us to redefine what it means to fail at school. The idea of playing in the sandbox with tools such as *Scratch* or *Minecraft* means that "failure" refers to something not working as expected. As Papert states in *Mindstorms*, the question is not whether the program is correct, but whether it is fixable. I think about my university experience studying computer science quite often. I was never asked to memorize syntax. Rather, we were provided syntax manuals and were asked to solve problems for other educational departments. This way of thinking, engaging in hard fun, showed me that failure will happen, and learning from failure is of utmost importance. Until we rethink what it means to fail in a math class, I am not entirely certain we can encourage young people to want to take risks.

There is tremendous risk in not getting good grades.

Humans will never embrace failure in a system in which failure is punished.

As a former physical education teacher, I am reminded of how students learn to make a layup or serve a volleyball.

Hard fun.

Trial and error.

Immediate feedback from the environment.

Why did I give bonus marks for active participation in my gym class?

Although this may not be the case everywhere, I certainly did it. I would also give marks if students came to class in uniform. I never once gave students math marks for showing up with a protractor, nor did effort play a role. Math grades were determined by a quantity of correctness

(Remember, it is okay to be where you are, and this is where I was at the time.).

Without calling it that at the time, my approach to instruction in physical education was hard fun. I pushed students out of their comfort zones, challenged their abilities, and encouraged them to get better. They were also motivated to do so because they believed in themselves.

That's the growth mindset at work, and it's the kind of mindset our students need in math class—and every other class for that matter.

Back to *Minecraft*. Much like my gym class, creating content in *Minecraft* allows students to ask questions, make predictions, try new things, make observations, and construct knowledge of mathematics and the world around them. Whether they are building structures to scale, developing roller coasters with redstone, or creating games that involve growing patterns, they are engaging in hard fun. This is a space that cannot be quantified to a single letter grade, which has me thinking a great deal about terms such as *progressive* and *traditional* when discussing education in general.

Simply using tools such as *Minecraft* does not make us "progressive" educators because it isn't about the tool. As I have mentioned, tools change. Real innovation lies in relationship building, providing endless opportunities for students to achieve, and being mindful about demographics, culture, and different ways of life. However, "traditional" teachers share these characteristics, so where have these terms come from? And, unfortunately, we often equate "traditional" to mean "bad."

***Minecraft* allows students to ask questions, make predictions, try new things, make observations, and construct knowledge of mathematics and the world around them.**

#BlockBreaker

Do I consider myself a progressive teacher? As often as possible. Do I consider myself a traditional teacher? Sure, sometimes. If we were to construct a giant Venn diagram of the two, I'd be somewhere in the middle. Where would you place yourself?

"Traditional" Education

- Teachers have knowledge to share with students
- Authoritative, in-charge, and lecture often
- Clear and distinct rules
- Quiet rows of desks
- Students take notes, mastery of skills
- Prepare for the "real world"
- Textbooks, workbooks, pencil, paper
- Rote, repetitive
- Grade motivated
- Standing teacher at front

"Progressive" Education

- Knowledge is everywhere, teachers are not experts
- Collaborative, student freedom, and self-taught
- Common-sense rules of life applied to classroom
- Student learning spaces
- Student performance to demonstrate learning
- "Real world" is an everyday component of class
- Student-created materials acquired from knowledge sources
- Open response
- Performance motivated
- Teacher sitting with students, much a part of learning spaces

This list STEMS (See what I did there?) from various sources online. It is quite binary in nature and reminds me of a toggle switch, as if you are one or the other. Off or on, black or white, zero or one. The use of quotations is intentional, and you can infer your own schema of what I am trying to suggest. Ultimately, we must ask ourselves the "why" when we are planning activities.

Chapter 9

0 0 1 1 1 0 0 1

Biting the Hand That Feeds Us: Rethinking Feedback

Play is often talked about as if it
were a relief from serious learning.
But for children, play is serious learning.
Play is really the work of childhood.
—Mr. Rogers

I love summer camp. The enthusiasm and energy of camp leaders is incredibly contagious. (I often wonder whether camp counsellor burnout is a thing as summer comes to a close much as teacher burnout is a thing during the school year.) Regardless, camp activities are carefully planned, and materials are sorted, packaged, and prepared for each session. Depending on the type of camp, campers receive merit badges for demonstrating skills—fire starting, cooking, coding, etc. And there are many ways to start a fire, cook, or code—and many skills involved. Countless articles on the internet call for school to be more like summer camp. As radical as it sounds, there may just be some merit (pun intended) to merit badges in school. After all, the word *merit* means good or worthy of praise for effort. Imagine a school system in which students could leave after receiving a certain number of badges and that no two students needed the same badges to graduate.

What if the goal were to obtain thirty badges, and you had hundreds to choose from to demonstrate learning while in school?

I don't claim to own this idea, as I have read it time and time again, but I do see how intrinsically motivating it could be for students. Some students are already intrinsically motivated by grades, but many don't care about a number on a page, particularly if they feel that number is unfair or arbitrary. But if they had a meaningful, authentic opportunity to demonstrate a skill, feel confidence, and be successful, I bet they'd care. Merit badges or not, I can certainly get behind an ungraded system that relies heavily on feedback alone to help keep kids moving.

What do merit badges have to do with the message of this book? If I have learned anything over the years about edtech tools, it is that proper implementation provides opportunities for all learners to feel some level of success and confidence, thus reducing any form of standardization. Sandbox tools such as *Scratch* or *Minecraft* are so naturally scaffolded, anyone can begin to create content seamlessly. Activities can be easily extended to match and challenge the skill level of each student. Open-ended projects are referred to as "low floor/high ceiling" with "wide walls," meaning all learners can approach the task (multiple entry points), and tasks can be extended to an almost infinite space for students who require more challenging activities.

My desire to incorporate *Minecraft* into my classroom began because a parent gave me great feedback. A distraught father knew his child was intelligent, but his son's report cards told another story. Those grades said his son wasn't measuring up to our standards, that he was dumb. Once I let this student use *Minecraft* to show his learning, I saw how much he knew. And if I'd had any merit badges to give away, he certainly would have earned them.

VOLCANO!

LEARNING GOAL

To learn about volcanoes and their effect on the planet

MINDS ON

Ask students what they know about the most recent volcano eruption in Hawaii. If possible, provide images and videos found online. Ask students what life must be like there and how it has changed.

LET'S EXPLORE

Have students research the size of certain volcanoes and their proximity to neighbourhood communities. Encourage students to design and build the same volcano in *Minecraft* to a certain scale. Encourage students to also build a representation of the neighbouring city and narrate what could happen in a potential disaster.

CONSOLIDATION

Ask students to simulate what could happen if their volcano erupted. Have them time how long it might take for lava to enter certain parts of the closest community. Have students present their *Minecraft* volcanoes to the class, and as a group, discuss the environmental impacts.

The person who changed the most during this time wasn't my student, however. He was already smart; he just needed a way to show his intelligence.

I learned the most. I learned to receive and respond to great feedback.

I've long been critical of current educational practices that focus on and prioritize letter grades and marks. I think these practices can discourage students from actively and creatively pursuing their own learning. I think they can cause us as educators to focus more on concepts than on the students we are teaching. Personally, I'd like to see the way we use grades reduced, or quite frankly, eliminated. This might sound radical, but it isn't. Educators have been questioning our assessment practices for decades. Research shows that educators from around the world have been concerned about the effectiveness and usefulness of grades for years.

I prefer to give constructive feedback instead of numerical grades.

Effective feedback includes knowing what you want students to achieve, what obstacles are keeping them from achieving that goal, and what they can do to overcome those obstacles. Our current system of assessment, with its focus on standardized testing, letter grades, percentages, and question-and-answer times between students and teachers, can actually be creating more obstacles to learning. Assessment is an obstacle that keeps our students from meeting the goal of doing better in education. Evaluation should not drive instruction. "I need a math mark" should be removed from our vocabulary because it dictates the type of lesson we will create, rather than focusing on the needs of the learner.

Students who feel valued will always perform better when faced with authentic problems. Kids want to impress you!

#BlockBreaker

The problems with our current forms of assessment have been well documented. Let me outline a few here. First, they often prioritize memorization of information more than the application of information. That's why I like *Minecraft* as an educational tool. Students learn and apply their knowledge at the same time. Second, they can encourage passive learning. Students, like everyone else, are more likely to do things that are easy and don't require a lot of effort.

When students think that all teachers want is just the "right" answer, that's what all students are going to give. They'll do this because true learning—which most often involves asking questions and finding new solutions, often through making mistakes—is hard. Students know whether they're "good" at the system or not. The mark they receive on a test or assignment may just reinforce what they already know to be true about themselves. These systems don't encourage growth or give students opportunities to try again and improve. Simply put, they end learning.

The purpose of constructive feedback is to encourage learning and growth.

Finally, the most concerning problem with these assessment models is they reduce students to marks. Educators often talk about how, in some ways, we are to be like parents to our students. But if a parent described their child simply in terms of their marks at school, we would think that they're a bad parent. By the same logic, we're not good teachers if we just describe students by their grades. The next time you are at a family barbeque, ask a relative how their child is doing.

You might hear something like, "Johnny can skate backwards now!"

This is more qualitative than quantitative. No ever says, "Jenny got a 72% on her last walking test!" The use of adjectives is so prevalent when describing our family members; why does it change when talking about students? There are many ways to give feedback that encourage students to learn, build on their existing skills, and develop new ones. This can be more than just giving students feedback about how they can improve an assignment and letting them hand it back to see whether they get a higher mark. That might be helpful in some cases, although I sometimes wonder whether this practice just strengthens the belief that the "best" work is the one that gets the highest mark.

Some teachers don't give marks at all.

Instead, they hand back assignments with questions on them that give students further things to think about or ways to improve their future work. Students engage better with this than with receiving letter grades. Perhaps most important, edtech tools such as *Minecraft* or *Scratch* help provide the user with immediate feedback. It either works or it doesn't.

Some teachers design their assessment tools in ways that teach students the concepts they want them to learn. They often do this by having the class work together to determine what type of assessment would be best for the material they're learning. This can help determine what students believe is the goal of the lesson, and as a result, how well they understand the material. Because students work as a team to design their assessments, they have to learn to listen to one another, provide feedback on each other's ideas, and come up with solutions.

One way to think of this is by using the idea of badges. Remember how kids at summer camp used to see how many badges they could collect? Badges work for many reasons. First, they give a visual reward for achievement. Students can clearly picture their goal. Second, the badge is connected to the community in a few different ways. Other people see the badge and recognize it. The badge also gives a picture of the skill the student mastered to earn the badge. But the badge is also designed by a community. Think about medals in the Olympics. The medal matters because a group of people—the International Olympic Committee—have agreed it does. I can't just declare myself a champion sprinter on my own by draping a gold circle on a string around my neck. It doesn't work that way. A committee has to decide what the standards are to receive badges. And finally, badges help motivate further learning. They take what may be considered ordinary or even eccentric hobbies and make them something worth pursuing and celebrating. Really—think of how the Boy Scouts turned knowing different types of knots into something to brag about years later!

Feedback is meant to motivate and encourage students. It's not supposed to be a way to judge teacher performance.

Really, it is about them. As with anything in teaching, the best way to teach our students is to model the behaviour we want them to demonstrate. As Alice Keeler said recently on Twitter: **"We don't need apps that make grading faster; we need apps that help give better feedback."**

And feedback can be conversations. Leaving comments as feedback on a doc is not as powerful as communicating directly in real time.

This book exists because a student's father gave me great feedback that day in the school office. He had a clear goal he wanted to accomplish: He wanted his son to finish elementary school on a successful note. He knew the obstacle that was keeping his son from completing that goal: a school system that highlighted his failures and not his successes. Finally, he knew what had to change for his son to reach the goal: how we taught his son.

"Why do you focus on his weaknesses when he will pursue his strengths in life?"

Hmm. Food for thought.

That year will forever hold a special place in my heart. Not only did this student begin participating in classroom activities, but his behaviour improved, and other students asked him for help with *Minecraft*. It was apparent to me that *Minecraft* was the perfect tool for him to demonstrate learning—something he had struggled to do without technology. I am reminded of the SAMR model developed by Dr. Ruben Puentedura. In this model, technology acts as a support and enhancement in a variety of ways.

- **Substitution:** Technology acts as a direct tool substitute without any functional change.
- **Augmentation:** Technology acts as a direct tool substitute with functional improvements.
- **Modification:** Technology allows for significant task redesign.
- **Redefinition:** Technology allows for the creation of new tasks, previously inconceivable.

Where would you place our *Minecraft* projects? Can you think of a lesson you have that SAMR could impact? The idea of modification and redefinition completely supports my theories regarding student choice and voice while leveling the playing field. I refer to open-ended student projects as "sandbox" approaches, and if we are to have students create content that was previously inconceivable, then grading cannot exist as it is, based on a concrete list of criteria and expectations rather than forward-thinking, previously unimaginable content.

Perhaps most important, this story isn't about the tool as much as it is about unlocking the student's potential that we knew he had. This story is about how a simple approach helped build confidence and success for an individual who didn't much care for school. Finally, this story is about how I improved my own practice just by simply listening to a parent.

Granted, I needed to respond to him appropriately. I had to take action. I did. I introduced his son to *Minecraft*. His son responded by using the game. He actually went beyond our expectations by pursuing knowledge about *Minecraft* outside of the classroom. I could have listened to what the father said and not changed a thing. I could have decided to stay rooted in my old ways of teaching, regardless of how that might have hurt my students. But I didn't. I chose to grow—to try something new in teaching. As I reflect on this experience, I am reminded of a quote from Dr. Kevin Maxwell: "**Our job is to teach the students we have. Not the ones we would like to have. Not the ones we used to have. Those we have right now. All of them.**"

Thank you to all the parents and educators out there who want what is best for all students. Thank you to that parent who made me cry early on in my teaching career, for you opened my eyes to the notion that all students can achieve if given a fair chance. Remember: Fairness is not sameness.

Trust me. All students can achieve if given a fair chance.

Chapter 10

0 1 0 1 1 0 0 0

My Secret Confession

The role of the teacher is to create the conditions for invention rather than provide ready-made knowledge.
—Seymour Papert

I have a confession. While I enjoy video games, I do not play *Minecraft* very much. I likely have about twenty minutes' playing time to my name. I know what you must be thinking:

WHAAAAT?

When I began teaching, I thought I had to know everything about tools and technology. I thought I had to be three steps ahead of the kids in my class with regard to the next best app. Student engagement, at the time, meant using all the bells and whistles I could pack into a PowerPoint presentation. I wore myself thin, teaching all day, planning lessons all night, and downloading apps in my sleep. It was not sustainable.

I no longer think this way.

My job is to know my curriculum really well and recognize teachable moments as they occur. I know what *Minecraft* is capable of, and I know how it fits my curriculum. I no longer worry about the next SnapGram or InstaChat. My classroom has flattened. No more hierarchies. I teach you, you teach me, and you teach you. I have come a long way since my first teaching assignment. In those days I would have spent countless hours playing *Minecraft,* so I could troubleshoot the tool and teach the tool.

Blah. I am so glad I have moved on!

Today I let my students fumble through the tool and teach each other in the process. My job is providing access to curriculum and being someone who cares for kids. Who I am as a teacher significantly outweighs what it is I teach. Kids will remember me as a person before they remember specific dates or formulas.

The next time you have to plan a professional development (PD) day, put up chart paper and ask teachers to reflect on their school experience. What do they remember about their favourite teacher? I guarantee it won't be about dates or formulas.

If I can offer kids a safe place to take risks, have conversations with them about their learning, and provide real-time feedback, I think I am doing okay. This approach makes learning authentic, and students can make sense of the curriculum.

We don't need to cover curriculum. We need to let students *uncover* it.

We need to let students *discover* it.

I will never forget that grade eight year. Remembering the smile on that blue-eyed autistic teenager's face as he created content for everyone to see still gives me goosebumps. In fact, the more I planned activities for his needs, the more I thought about everyone's needs, and the more time I took to get to know every student. For that I am grateful.

The real 1:1 is more about personal connections we make with every student and less about the number of devices our classrooms have.

#BlockBreaker

Knowing who our students are helps us direct lesson activities. Knowing about student interests, problems, and family life helps build a tremendous positive culture and rapport. Program determines behaviour, and a positive culture enables a safe place for students to take risks without fear or the feeling of vulnerability. Students who like you will do their best to impress you. I have come a long way in my own practice, but I'd be naive to think there still isn't more work to be done.

It is okay to be where you are.

It is *not* okay to stay there.

References

0 1 0 1 0 0 1 0

"Quotes by Dr. Kevin Maxwell." *Bam!Radio.* Accessed February 25, 2019. http://www.bamradionetwork.com/quoted/author_quotes/8-dr-kevin-maxwell.

Berry, Miles. *Computing in the National Curriculum. A Guide for Primary Teachers.* Bedford, UK: Computing at School, 2013.

Bers, Marina Umaschi, Louise Flannery, Elizabeth R. Kazako, and Amanda Sullivan. "Computational Thinking and Tinkering: Exploration of an Early Childhood Robotics Curriculum." *Computers & Education* 72, (2014):145–57. doi:10.1016/j.compedu.2013.10.020.

Drake, Susan M. "Designing across the Curriculum for "Sustainable Well-Being": A 21st Century Approach." In *Sustainable Well-Being: Concepts, Issues, and Educational Practice,* edited by Frank Deer, Thomas Falkenberg, Barbara McMillan, and Laura Sims, 57–76. Winnipeg, MB: Education for Sustainable Well-Being (ESWB) Press, 2014. http://www.eswb-press.org/uploads/1/2/8/9/12899389/sustainable_well-being_2014.pdf#page=65.

Fullan, Michael. "Great to Excellent: Launching the Next State of Ontario's Education Agenda." *Motion Leadership.* 2013. http://www.michaelfullan.ca/wp-content/uploads/2013/09/13_Fullan_Great-to-Excellent.pdf.

Gadanidis, George. "Why can't I be a mathematician?" *For the Learning of Mathematics* 32, no. 2 (July 2012): 20–6. http://researchideas.ca/documents/05-Gadanidis.pdf.

Gadanidis, George. "Coding as a Trojan Horse for Mathematics Education Reform." *Journal of Computers in Mathematics and Science Teaching* 34, no. 2 (2015): 155–173.

Gadanidis, George. *Coding for Young Mathematicians.* London, Ontario, Canada: Western University, 2015.

Gao, Xin, and Jennifer Grisham-Brown. "The Use of Authentic Assessment to Report Accountability Data on Young Children's Language, Literacy and Pre-Math Competency." *International Education Studies* 4, no. 2 (2011). doi:10.5539/ies.v4n2p41.

Graf, Edith Aurora, and Meirav Arieli-Aali. "Designing and Developing Assessments of Complex Thinking in Mathematics for the Middle Grades." *Theory into Practice* 54, no. 3 (2015): 195–202. doi:10.1080/00405841.2015.1044365.

Hargreaves, Eleanore. "Mathematics Assessment for Children with English as an Additional Language." *Assessment in Education: Principles, Policy & Practice* 4, no. 3 (1997): 401–412. doi:10.1080/0969594970040306.

Harlen, Wynne, and Jan Winter. "The Development of Assessment for Learning: Learning from the Case of Science and Mathematics." *Language Testing* 21, no. 3 (2004): 390–408. doi:10.1191/0265532204lt289oa.

Jeltova, Ida, Damian Birney, Nancy Fredine, Linda Jarvin, Robert J. Sternberg, and Elena L. Grigorenko. "Making Instruction and Assessment Responsive to Diverse Students' Progress: Group-Administered Dynamic Assessment in Teaching Mathematics." *Journal of Learning Disabilities* 44, no. 4 (2011): 381–395. doi:10.1177/0022219411407868.

Kafai, Yasmin B., and Quinn Burke. "Computer Programming Goes Back to School." *Phi Delta Kappan* 95, no. 1 (2013): 63–65.

Kazako, Elizabeth R., and Marina Umaschi Bers. "Put Your Robot in, Put Your Robot out: Sequencing through Programming Robots in Early Childhood." *Journal of Educational Computing Research* 50, no. 4 (2014): 553–73. doi:10.2190/ec.50.4.f.

Kazako, Elizabeth R., Amanda Sullivan, and Marina U. Bers. "The Effect of a Classroom-Based Intensive Robotics and Programming Workshop on Sequencing Ability in Early Childhood." *Early Childhood Education Journal* 41, no. 4 (2012): 245–55. doi:10.1007/ s10643-012-0554-5.

"Creativity and Education." *Knowledge Without Borders*. February 6, 2014. http://knowwithoutborders.org/creativity-education.

Levine, Rachel. "Curriculum-based Dynamic Assessment Emphasizing a Triarchic Model and Language Abilities: Examining the Utility of This Testing Method in Elementary School Mathematics Classrooms." PhD diss., Farleigh Dickinson University, New Jersey, 2009. (Order No. 3349141). *ProQuest Education Journals*. (305047877). http://search.proquest.com/docview/305047877?accountid=15115.

Liang, Xin. "Assessment Use, Self-efficacy and Mathematics Achievement: Comparative Analysis of PISA 2003 Data of Finland, Canada and the USA." *Evaluation & Research in Education* 23, no. 3 (2010): 213–29. Accessed February 25, 2019. http://search.proquest.com/docview/868061586?accountid=15115.

Misfeldt, Morten, and Stine Ejsing-Duun. "Learning Mathematics through Programming: An Instrumental Approach to Potentials and Pitfalls." In *Proceedings of the Ninth Congress of the European Society For Research in Mathematics Education*, edited by Konrad Krainer and Nada Vondrova, 2524-2530. Prague, Czech Republic: Charles University of Prague, Faculty of Education and ERME, 2015.

Morgan, Candia, Anna Tsatsaroni, and Stephen Lerman. "Mathematics Teachers' Positions and Practices in Discourses of Assessment." *British Journal of Sociology of Education* 23, no. 3 (2002): 445–461. Accessed February 25, 2019. http://search.proquest.com/docview/206172116?accountid=15115.

Nguyen, Diem M, Yi-Chuan Hsieh, and Donald G Allen. "The Impact of Web-Based Assessment and Practice on Students' Mathematics Learning Attitudes." *Journal of Computers in Mathematics and Science Teaching* 25, no. 3 (2006): 251–279. Accessed February 25, 2019. http://search.proquest.com/docview/220630959?accountid=15115.

"21st Century Competencies: Foundation Document for Discussion." EduGAINS, 2015. http://www.edugains.ca/resources21CL/About21stCentury/21CL_21stCenturyCompetencies.pdf.

"The Ontario Curriculum Grades 1-8: Mathematics." Ontario Ministry of Education, 2005. http://www.edu.gov.on.ca/eng/curriculum/elementary/math18curr.pdf.

Papert, Seymour. "Turtle geometry: A mathematics made for learning." Chap. 3 in *Mindstorms: Children, Computers, and Powerful Ideas*. New York: Basicbooks, 1993.

Puentedura, Ruben R. "SMAR: A Brief Intro." *Hippasus* (blog), 2015, Accessed February 25, 2019. http://hippasus.com/rrpweblog/archives/2015/10/SAMR_ABriefIntro.pdf.

Resnick, Mitchel, John Maloney, Andrés Monroy-Hernández, Natalie Rusk, Evelyn Eastmond, Karen Brennan, Amon Millner, et al. "'Digital Fluency' Should Mean Designing, Creating, and Remixing, Not Just Browsing, Chatting, and Interacting." *Communications of the ACM* 52, no. 11 (2009): 60–7.

Sammons, Kay, et al. "Linking Instruction and Assessment in the Mathematics Classroom." *The Arithmetic Teacher* 39, no. 6 (1992): 11. Accessed February 25, 2019. http://search.proquest.com/docview/208771651?accountid=15115.

Singh, Sunil. *Pi of Life*. London: Rowman & Littlefield, 2017.

Smith, Carmen Petrick, and Maureen D. Neumann. "Scratch It Out! Enhancing Geometrical Understanding." *Teaching Children Mathematics* 21, no. 3 (2014): 185–188.

Sneider, Cary, Chris Stephenson, Bruce Schafer, and Larry Flick. "Teachers Toolkit: Exploring the Science Framework and NGSS: Computational Thinking in the Science Classroom." *Science Scope* 038, no. 03 (2014): 10–15.

Suurtamm, Christine, and Martha J. Koch. "Navigating Dilemmas in Transforming Assessment Practices: Experiences of Mathematics Teachers in Ontario, Canada." *Educational Assessment, Evaluation and Accountability* 26, no. 3 (2014): 263–287. doi:10.1007/s11092-014-9195-0.

Suurtamm, Christine, Martha Koch, and Ann Arden. "Teachers' Assessment Practices in Mathematics: Classrooms in the Context of Reform." *Assessment in Education: Principles, Policy & Practice* 17, no. 4 (2010): 399–417. Accessed February 25, 2019. http://search.proquest.com/docview/821956768?accountid=15115.

Thomas, Cathy Newman, Delinda Van Garderen, Amy Scheuermann, and Eun Ju Lee. "Applying a Universal Design for Learning Framework to Mediate the Language Demands of Mathematics." *Reading & Writing Quarterly* 31, no. 3 (2015): 207–234. Accessed February 25, 2019. http://search.proquest.com/docview/1683616180?accountid=15115.

Wallace, Mayhew. "Developing Assessment Practices: a Study of the Experiences of Preservice Mathematics Teachers as Learners and the Evolution of Their Assessment Practices as Educators." PhD diss., (3499583). Farleigh Dickinson University, New Jersey, 2011. *ProQuest Education Journals* (944324214). http://search.proquest.com/docview/944324214?accountid=15115.

Watson, Anne. "Some Difficulties in Informal Assessment in Mathematics." *Assessment in Education: Principles, Policy & Practice* 13, no. 3 (2006): 289–303. Accessed February 25, 2019. http://search.proquest.com/docview/204048130?accountid=15115.

Wing, Jeannee. "Computational Thinking." *Communications of the ACM* 49, no. 3 (2006): 33–35. Accessed February 25, 2019. http://www.cs.cmu.edu/afs/cs/usr/wing/www/publications/Wing06.pdf.

Yin, Yue, Judith Olson, Melfried Olson, Hannah Solvin, and Paul R. Brandon. "Comparing Two Versions of Professional Development for Teachers Using Formative Assessment in Networked Mathematics Classrooms." *Journal of Research on Technology in Education* 47, no. 1 (2015): 41–70. Accessed February 25, 2019. http://search.proquest.com/docview/1646385125?accountid=15115.

Bring Brian Aspinall to Your School or Event

0 1 0 0 0 0 1 0

Twenty-first-century learning requires students to create, collaborate, and think critically. Progress "STEMs" directly from immediate feedback and a personalized learning platform. Coding forces students to problem solve, make mistakes, and overcome barriers because programs can only run if written correctly. In this workshop, teachers will learn the basics of block-based coding and how to make use of mathematical principles to create content for learning.

In this workshop, participants will learn about the history and pedagogy of computer science, its importance for the future, and how to integrate it into existing curricula. With a focus on twenty-first-century competencies, participants will explore assessment and evaluation while engaging in the process of learning.

Brian is an elementary teacher and university instructor on a mission to expose as many kids as he can to coding and computer science. In this passionate talk, he makes a case for the importance of exposing youth to the principles of coding and computational thinking to prepare them for a rapidly changing future.

More from Brian:

TEDx Talks

Beyond Rote Learning (Chatham, ON)
Published March 14, 2014

Education Reform (Chatham, ON)
Published June 16, 2015

Hacking the Classroom (Kitchener, ON)
Published June 16, 2016

http://brianaspinall.com/tedx-talks

Aside from being an educator, instructor, and consultant, Brian has been developing apps since the early 1990s, when his high school principal paid him to develop the school's first website.

Unfortunately, neither the website nor the high school still exist.

Gone But Not Forgotten

View the blog:

http://brianaspinall.com/ to-the-students-of-harrow-district-high-school

To find out more about Brian Aspinall and his body of work, visit:

http://www.mraspinall.com

http://www.brianaspinall.com

Follow Brian:

On Twitter (@mraspinall)

On Instagram (@mr.aspinall)

More From Dave Burgess Consulting, Inc.

Since 2012, DBCI has been publishing books that inspire and equip educators to be their best. For more information on our DBCI titles or to purchase bulk orders for your school, district, or book study, visit DaveBurgessconsulting.com/DBCIbooks.

More from the PIRATE™ Series

Teach Like a PIRATE by Dave Burgess
eXPlore Like a Pirate by Michael Matera
Learn Like a Pirate by Paul Solarz
Play Like a Pirate by Quinn Rollins
Run Like a Pirate by Adam Welcome

Lead Like a PIRATE™ Series

Lead Like a PIRATE by Shelley Burgess and Beth Houf
Balance Like a Pirate by Jessica Cabeen, Jessica Johnson, and Sarah Johnson
Lead beyond Your Title by Nili Bartley
Lead with Culture by Jay Billy
Lead with Literacy by Mandy Ellis

Leadership & School Culture

Culturize by Jimmy Casas

Escaping the School Leader's Dunk Tank by Rebecca Coda and Rick Jetter

From Teacher to Leader by Starr Sackstein

The Innovator's Mindset by George Couros

Kids Deserve It! by Todd Nesloney and Adam Welcome

Let Them Speak by Rebecca Coda and Rick Jetter

The Limitless School by Abe Hege and Adam Dovico

The Pepper Effect by Sean Gaillard

The Principled Principal by Jeffrey Zoul and Anthony McConnell

The Secret Solution by Todd Whitaker, Sam Miller, and Ryan Donlan

Start. Right. Now. by Todd Whitaker, Jeffrey Zoul, and Jimmy Casas

Stop. Right. Now. by Jimmy Casas and Jeffrey Zoul

Unmapped Potential by Julie Hasson and Missy Lennard

They Call Me "Mr. De" by Frank DeAngelis

Your School Rocks by Ryan McLane and Eric Lowe

Technology & Tools

50 Things You Can Do with Google Classroom by Alice Keeler and Libbi Miller

50 Things to Go Further with Google Classroom by Alice Keeler and Libbi Miller

140 Twitter Tips for Educators by Brad Currie, Billy Krakower, and Scott Rocco

Code Breaker by Brian Aspinall

Google Apps for Littles by Christine Pinto and Alice Keeler

Master the Media by Julie Smith

Shake Up Learning by Kasey Bell

Social LEADia by Jennifer Casa-Todd

Teaching Math with Google Apps by Alice Keeler and Diana Herrington

Teaching Methods & Materials

All 4s and 5s by Andrew Sharos

Ditch That Homework by Matt Miller and Alice Keeler

Ditch That Textbook by Matt Miller

Educated by Design by Michael Cohen, The Tech Rabbi

The EduProtocol Field Guide by Marlena Hebern and Jon Corippo

Instant Relevance by Denis Sheeran

LAUNCH by John Spencer and A.J. Juliani

Make Learning MAGICAL by Tisha Richmond

Pure Genius by Don Wettrick

Shift This! by Joy Kirr

Spark Learning by Ramsey Musallam

Sparks in the Dark by Travis Crowder and Todd Nesloney

Table Talk Math by John Stevens

The Classroom Chef by John Stevens and Matt Vaudrey

The Wild Card by Hope and Wade King

The Writing on the Classroom Wall by Steve Wyborney

Inspiration, Professional Growth & Personal Development

The Four O'Clock Faculty by Rich Czyz

Be REAL by Tara Martin

Be the One for Kids by Ryan Sheehy

Creatively Productive by Lisa Johnson

The EduNinja Mindset by Jennifer Burdis

How Much Water do We Have? by Pete and Kris Nunweiler

P Is for Pirate by Dave and Shelley Burgess

A Passion for Kindness by Tamara Letter

The Path to Serendipity by Allyson Apsey

Sanctuaries by Dan Tricarico

Shattering the Perfect Teacher Myth by Aaron Hogan

Stories from Webb by Todd Nesloney

Talk to Me by Kim Bearden

The Zen Teacher by Dan Tricarico

Children's Books

Dolphins in Trees by Aaron Polansky

The Princes of Serendip by Allyson Apsey

Also from Brian Aspinall

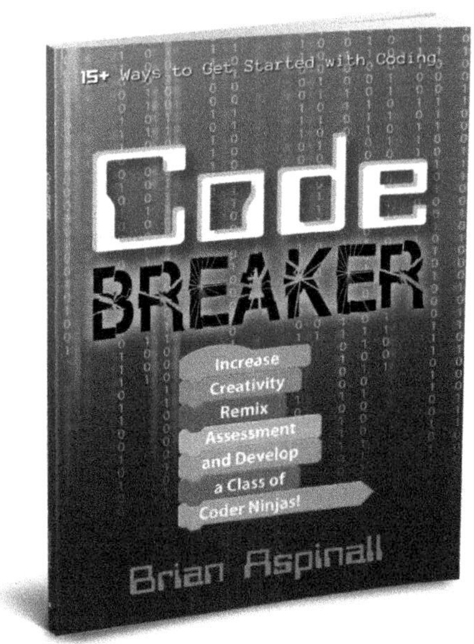

Code Breaker

Increase Creativity, Remix Assessment, and Develop a Class of Coder Ninjas!

Code Breaker equips you to use coding in your classroom to turn curriculum expectations into skills. Students learn how to identify problems, develop solutions, and use computational thinking to apply and demonstrate their learning. Best of all, you don't have to be a "computer geek" to empower your students with these essential skills.

About the Author

0 1 0 0 0 0 0 1

Brian Aspinall is an educator and best-selling author who is considered one of the brightest STEM innovators in Canadian education. His book, *Code Breaker: 15+ Ways to Get Started with Coding,* continues to top the charts in STEM education with a focus on rethinking assessment and evaluation. Recently he was awarded the Prime Minister's Award for Teaching Excellence for his work with coding and computational thinking. His enthusiasm, thought leadership, and approach to building capacity within STEM education has made him a sought-after speaker throughout North America and has earned him the honour of being selected as Canada's first *Minecraft,* Micro:Bit, and Makey Makey Ambassador!

CPSIA information can be obtained
at www.ICGtesting.com
Printed in the USA
FSHW011630220319
56540FS